## EXTRA! EXTRA!

# EAT ALL ABOUT IT!

## Recipes and Culinary Curiosities from Historic Wisconsin Newspapers

# EXTRA! EXTRA!
# EAT ALL ABOUT IT!

Recipes and Culinary Curiosities
from Historic Wisconsin Newspapers

## JANE CONWAY AND RANDI JULIA RAMSDEN

WISCONSIN HISTORICAL SOCIETY PRESS

Published by the Wisconsin Historical Society Press
*Publishers since 1855*

The Wisconsin Historical Society helps people connect to the past by collecting, preserving, and sharing stories. Founded in 1846, the Society is one of the nation's finest historical institutions.

*Join the Wisconsin Historical Society:* wisconsinhistory.org/membership

Photographs identified with WHi or WHS are from the Society's collections; address requests to reproduce these photos to the Visual Materials Archivist at the Wisconsin Historical Society, 816 State Street, Madison, WI 53706.

Front cover plate photo: Mark R. Coons/Shutterstock.com

Unless otherwise noted, all color photographs in the book were provided courtesy of the authors. All black and white engravings and electrotyped cuts are from General Catalog Number Twenty-Six of Stock Cuts for All Lines of Business, Milwaukee: C.R. Gether Company, 1907.

Printed in the United States of America
Cover design, text design, and typesetting by Steve Biel Design

28 27 26 25 24   1 2 3 4 5

Library of Congress Cataloging-in-Publication Data
Names: Conway, Jane, 1995– author. | Ramsden, Randi Julia, 1991– author.
Title: Extra! extra! eat all about it! : recipes and culinary curiosities from historic Wisconsin newspapers / Jane Conway and Randi Julia Ramsden.
Other titles: Eat all about it!
Description: First edition. | Madison, WI : Wisconsin Historical Society Press, [2024] | Includes index.
Identifiers: LCCN 2024005814 (print) | LCCN 2024005815 (ebook) | ISBN 9781976600371 (paperback) | ISBN 9781976600388 (ebook)
Subjects: LCSH: Cooking, American. | Cooking—Wisconsin. | LCGFT: Cookbooks.
Classification: LCC TX715 .C75885 2024 (print) | LCC TX715 (ebook) | DDC 641.59775—dc23/eng/20240228
LC record available at https://lccn.loc.gov/2024005814
LC ebook record available at https://lccn.loc.gov/2024005815

♾ The paper used in this publication meets the minimum requirements of the American National Standard for Information Sciences—Permanence of Paper for Printed Library Materials, ANSI Z39.48-1992.

*To the Sunday night dinner crew—Eli, John, Kaleb, Madita,*
*Maureen, and Paden—for fearlessly volunteering your taste buds*
*and joining us on this culinary adventure.*

# CONTENTS

# INTRODUCTION

The idea for this book sprouted in 2019 while we worked as colleagues at the Wisconsin Historical Society. Our job was to inspect thousands of historic newspaper pages for Chronicling America, a historic newspaper database developed and run by the National Digital Newspaper Program. Newspapers were once *the* medium covering current events, and they served as the principal source of education and entertainment for many. Working closely with local newspapers, we followed historical news stories, local events, community interests, and opinions as they unfolded. Alongside the familiar news items and articles, we also began noticing many columns dedicated to the home and garden, which often included recipes. Unlike cookbooks, which tend to be curated and refined over long periods, newspapers have always been able to publish recipes quickly, thereby capturing the culinary trends of specific moments in time. The newspaper recipes also revealed the tastes and traditions of a wide range of Wisconsinites. The majority of newspapers published in the state, including immigrant newspapers, as well as publications by local American Indian and African American communities, served quite small readerships and, therefore, offer insight into local culinary habits. While some recipes were clearly developed by professionals, others were submitted by community members.

Until digitization and the rise of the keyword search function in the last decade of the twentieth century, there was no easy way to access historical newspaper recipes, let alone search a wide swath of them for common themes. As we began taking note of recurring dishes and cooking fads, our excitement about this underutilized collection grew. The fact that the recipes had no accompanying images and existed merely as typed instructions intrigued us even further. We wanted to see what Wisconsinites used to eat; we wanted to get a taste of history ourselves.

The idea continued to marinate until we finally decided to attempt a recipe. One of our first experiments, in February 2020, involved parboiling onions, stuffing them

One of our first historical cooking experiments: stuffed onions cooked in a paper bag.

with meat, and baking them in a paper bag as per 1912 instructions. The result was surprisingly delicious. This recipe remains one of our favorites and has made it into this book (see "Paper Bag Cooking" on page 96). Following the success of our first culinary time-travel journey, we began to meet up regularly to browse historical recipes and cook.

Soon the COVID-19 pandemic confined us to our respective houses, but we did not want to let our new hobby go. Thanks to video conferencing technology, we were able to continue cooking together virtually, navigating and discussing the steps in each recipe through our phones and computers. Some of our friends joined these sessions, witnessing, for example, our struggles as we attempted to press beans through a sieve for a 1921 cheesy bean loaf.

With every pot we stirred, every ingredient we added to our shopping lists, and every bite we took, we learned something new. At the same time, we formulated many new questions: Should we be using our stand mixers? When did they become available, anyway? How did the coconut find its way to Wisconsin and end up on an 1888 cake? Why doesn't this recipe call for more spices? What does it mean to cook something in a "quick oven"? As history professionals, we could not help but go down the many rabbit holes that soon presented themselves. The same newspapers housing the recipes we re-created became the main sources for our research. Ads for ingredients and kitchen gadgets showed us what was available to people at the time, while exposés and reportage from correspondents allowed us to trace market developments and industry practices. In this process, we began compiling the materials that eventually formed this book, which is not merely a cookbook of recipes collected by two cooking enthusiasts (who are definitely not professional chefs) but also a compilation of historical essays revealing all that we have learned.

Using newspapers published in Wisconsin between the 1840s and the 1920s, which have now entered the public domain, we browsed hundreds of recipes that sparked our interest, while avoiding those that we did not feel comfortable ingesting ourselves or serving to our taste-testing friends, who are not usually picky eaters. We apologize, in advance, for what you may see as notable oversights; for instance, there is no gelatin recipe, despite people asking about it every time we revealed what we were working on. We also refrained from including recipes now commonly known to be poisonous, like sautéed rhubarb greens. On the other hand, we decided not to add instructions to pasteurize eggs in recipes calling for raw eggs. This should, however, not discourage you from doing so if you choose. The majority of the recipes in these pages will likely seem unusual to the contemporary palate. The casual addition of oysters to a beefsteak, for example, is no longer a common practice. We were similarly caught off guard by instructions to marinate maraschino cherries and grapefruit in an herb-infused dressing for a salad, but that dish turned out to be strangely tasty. In selecting the fifty dishes featured in this book, our goal was to curate a collection of recipes that would encourage people to try historical cooking and have fun in the process.

We chose some recipes because they call for ingredients local to Wisconsin, such as freshwater fish and cherries; others feature bananas or chocolate, and the accompanying essays allowed us to highlight the globalization that was already in full swing at the time. We also took the liberty of making minor changes to the recipes we chose. We converted measurements to current US customary standard units to spare you the headache of attempting the conversions themselves. We added the occasional pinch of salt and spice to some recipes—just enough to enhance tastes and aromas, but not so much as to completely alter the flavor profiles. We also suggested you use a food processor or mixer for convenience. However, each chapter includes an original recipe clipping alongside our modernized version, giving you the opportunity to see what we have changed, disagree with our interpretations, and take matters into your own hands. Also, thanks to Chronicling America, you can access each original recipe online using the links in the Notes section.

While these recipes come from many communities around the state, they do not necessarily reflect the traditional food cultures of those communities—one example is the Hungarian Salad published in the Ojibwe *Odanah Star*. Newspapers were more likely to print cooking trends and twists on popular dishes than ordinary staples already being cooked in local kitchens.

Although we did the bulk of the research for this book in our home kitchens, this project also took us on the road. We had the opportunity to cook in three different historical kitchens at Old World Wisconsin in the summer of 2021, where we learned about the logistics of cooking without kitchen counters, modern ventilation systems, and electricity. In rural Wisconsin, we visited two lovely apiarists, harvested honey, and discovered that at least one of us is definitely not allergic to bee stings. We attended maple syrup festivals and were taught traditional and modern techniques used by local

American Indian nations to process the sap. Our vacations became chances to explore more cooking traditions. A cabin stay turned into a series of experiments with historical camping recipes, including one that resulted in exploding eggs. No serious harm was done, but we picked many a shell fragment out of our hair that night. Our research was also not confined to the borders of Wisconsin. We picked heirloom apples planted by early homesteaders in the Appalachians in West Virginia to study apple varieties and how they have changed. A trip to Mexico was shaped by excursions to trace the origins of cacao and attempts to harvest and process coconuts in their various stages.

While researching, writing, and cooking for this book, we gained not just knowledge but also confidence in the kitchen—and a deeper appreciation for the food cultures that have influenced Wisconsin cuisine. We learned that cooking is not about perfection or authenticity, and that preparing a meal can be an exercise in exploring history.

If you picked up this book to learn about local food history, we hope that you will be inspired to try out a recipe in your own kitchen. If you came here to prepare an Apple de Luxe, we hope our historical essays help you pass the time while you wait for the oven to preheat. No matter the reason you were drawn to this book, we're glad you are here to join us on this culinary adventure through time.

# BREAKFAST AND BRUNCH

# 1
# BREAKFAST PARTIES

## Socializing at the Turn of the Century

In today's world, brunch is king in the realm of social breakfast gatherings, but, for a brief period, "breakfast parties" ruled as most popular in Wisconsin. Instead of planning a leisurely midday meal, party hosts would organize, cook, and prepare an entire breakfast for a group of friends early in the morning. Receiving guests near the crack of dawn was apparently not a problem for Ms. Theodora Axelberg from Washburn. On April 12, 1911, she "entertained twelve friends at an 8 o'clock breakfast party."[1]

Breakfast parties like Ms. Axelberg's started to appear in Wisconsin newspapers' social columns around the turn of the twentieth century, and the newfangled fad soon caught on across the state. Wisconsinites eagerly participated in the trend as it continued into the 1920s, with papers reporting, "Mrs. A. H. Clark entertained a company of lady friends at a breakfast party Wednesday," "a surprise breakfast party was given Miss Nelly in honor of her Birthday," and "Mrs. H. G. Stith was hostess at a breakfast party Monday A.M."[2] Often, social columns would mention not only the hostess but also the guests who attended these events. If you were not mentioned in the columns as either hosting or attending one of these popular parties, you must have been quite out of the loop, as far as this social trend was concerned.

Although most breakfast parties took place at a hostess's home, some were held in the great outdoors. In 1922, Mineral Point women were seen having breakfast gatherings at the Soldiers Memorial Park and Lake.[3] In Wausau, Rothschild Park was the venue chosen by Miss Isabelle Walker and her friends for a breakfast party followed by a dip in the river.[4]

Dishes that could be easily served in individual portions proved most popular for these occasions. An 1887 article in the *Mineral Point Tribune* listed shirred eggs as one of the "approved courses" for breakfast parties as they were prepared in individual dishes and could be served at both indoor and outdoor functions without difficulty.[5] Dishes that did not need to be portioned out were the most practical for hosts, especially when catering to a large group. A fried egg sandwich would also have fit the bill. When sliced in half, these delectable sandwiches can easily be distributed among guests. Even better, the filling can be prepared the night before a gathering, saving the cook precious time and energy in the morning.

With the right preparation, breakfast parties can be fun even for those who claim not to be morning people. They may even be pleasantly surprised by the experience. As Sydney Smith put it in the *River Falls Journal*, "I like breakfast parties, because no one is conceited before one o'clock in the day."[6]

# Fried Egg Sandwiches

*Watertown Weekly Leader,* June 1, 1915[7]

Makes 4 servings

## Fritter Batter[8]

1 cup flour

1 egg

2/3 cup milk

1 teaspoon salt

## Sandwiches

4 hard-boiled eggs

3 tablespoons butter, divided

2 tablespoons cream

Salt and black pepper, to taste

Paprika, to taste

4–6 small kaiser rolls

Oil, for frying

> Fried Egg Sandwiches.—Take two tablespoonfuls of butter, four hard-cooked eggs, two tablespoonfuls of cream, salt, pepper and paprika to taste. Pound the hard-cooked eggs to a paste, with the butter and cream, season well. Cut rolls into thin slices, butter them, spread with the mixture and make into small sandwiches. Dip each sandwich into a fritter batter and fry a golden brown. Serve hot.

For fritter batter: In a bowl, combine flour, egg, milk, and salt. Beat until smooth. Set aside.

For sandwiches: Pound the hard-boiled eggs to a paste, add 2 tablespoons of butter and the cream, and season with salt, pepper, and paprika. Cut kaiser rolls vertically, as you would a loaf of bread, into 1/2-inch slices. Each roll should make about 4 slices. Butter the slices with the remaining 1 tablespoon butter, and spread them with the egg mixture to make around two small, closed sandwiches per roll.

Dip each sandwich, top and bottom, into the fritter batter. Don't worry about coating the sides of the sandwich with batter, as it will run down the sides while frying.

Heat oil (1/4-inch deep) in a pan and fry the dipped sandwiches to a golden brown. Serve hot.

# 2

# À LA MODE AND OUH LÀ LÀ

## French Influences in Wisconsin Kitchens

As many Americans welcomed soldiers back from Europe following the end of the Great War, cooking columnist Biddy Bye observed something else arriving from France: recipes.[1] While culinary Francophilia may have been a postwar trend, it was not the first time that Wisconsinites tried their hand at dishes inspired by French cuisine. Home cooks had long been using recipes described as "French" as a way to make their dishes seem more prestigious, not necessarily due to their expensive components but rather because of the way they were processed. "A French cook turns any and every thing to advantage, and many a culinary chef d'oeuvre is the result of care and skill rather than rare or costly ingredients," stated a 1904 article in Edgerton's *Wisconsin Tobacco Reporter*. "With just a pinch of savory herbs and a clear fire a cook will turn shreds of cold meat into deliciously appetizing morsels."[2]

French recipes, or those described as such in Wisconsin newspapers, encouraged readers to experiment. An 1871 recipe with the bold title "French Soup MADE WITH-OUT MEAT" seems to have been notable because it derived most of its flavor from a combination of different herbs such as sorrel, mint, thyme, parsley, and cress.[3] In 1909, "an elaborate French recipe" for a Hollandaise sauce made with blood orange juice was featured as one of "Two Fancy Summer Dishes" in the *Grant County Herald*.[4] In many cases, the word *French* painted the dish as a delicacy, a decadent treat, or something superior and more complicated than dishes readers might usually prepare. According to the *River Falls Times*, one could give hot chocolate a French twist by adding an egg yolk to create an even richer beverage.[5]

In contrast, the use of *French* as a descriptor applied to kitchen tips and tricks was meant to assure readers of their safety and simplicity. In 1847, for example, the *Southport Telegraph* presented a French way of making rancid butter "fresh and sweet" by washing it with water and "thirty drops of [chloride] of lime," promising that this French practice was "safe and simple."[6] Nearly five decades later, the *Watertown Republican* taught readers an "old French recipe for removing grease-spots in silk," because who would know better how to care for delicate fabric than the inventors of haute couture?[7] And the French were surely to be trusted when it came to perfuming, as a 1906 recipe for bath sachets in the *Wood County Reporter* suggested. It called for bran, orris root, almond meal, and "good white soap."[8]

While Wisconsin kitchens continued to be influenced by the French well into the late 1800s, some home cooks worried that the trend would soon come to an end. In 1897, the *Manitowoc Pilot* warned that the "hurry and anxiety of modern life is slowly destroying whatever was distinctive in French cooking, which cannot be properly done in haste or when food is required in very large quantities."[9] Luckily, the hustle and bustle of the turn of the century did not cause the demise of French cuisine in France or Wisconsin, and newspapers continued to provide French-inspired amuse-bouches.

# *Eggs à la Mode*

*Wisconsin Weekly Blade*, June 12, 1919[10]

Makes 4 servings

4 slices bread

4 eggs

3 tablespoons butter, divided

¼ teaspoon paprika

Salt and black pepper, to taste

2 tablespoons white vinegar

1 teaspoon fresh parsley

Toast round slices of bread. A wide-mouthed canning jar band can be used to cut the bread into circular shapes.

Fry eggs in 1 tablespoon butter that has not been allowed to brown. The eggs may be cooked in the canning jar band to give them a circular shape. Season with paprika, salt, and pepper.

For sauce: Melt the remaining 2 tablespoons butter and stir until browned. Add vinegar and chopped parsley.

Place the fried eggs on the toast and pour sauce over the eggs.

## EGGS A LA MODE; THAT IS, FRENCH

### BY BIDDY BYE

Styles have come from France, soldiers are coming constantly—and now recipes from French kitchens once more are beginning to creep thru the lines.

As a starter, two cheering ways to transform familiar, American egg dishes, have reached our ears. We might crudely call them veal omelet and fried eggs on toast—but this is what happens in the making:

Make an omelet of 3 eggs, not stiffly beaten, seasoned with 1-2 teaspoonful of salt, not more than 1-4 that amount of pepper, and mixed with 3 tablespoonfuls of of water. Let it stand until cold, after cooking well in a buttered pan. Take 2 large thin slices of veal, cut the omelet in two slices, and roll each slice of omelet inside a slice of veal. When rolled, it can be tied with a string or held together with a toothpick. Saute the rolls in a buttered frying pan, letting them brown on all sides. When serving, pour over them on the platter a butter gravy, to which has been added a little Worcestershire sauce.

Now for the fried eggs, first toast round slices of bread and put them, buttered, in a warm oven. Fry the eggs in butter which has not been allowed to brown. When fried, put them on the pieces of toast, trimming each egg to a round shape to fit the toast. The completing touch is the making of a sauce, of 2 tablespoonfuls of butter, melted and stirred until it is a decided brown, a teaspoonful of chopped parsley, and 2 tablespoonfuls of vinegar. Paprika, salt and pepper dashed over the eggs, and the sauce poured on— and they are ready to serve.

# 3

# WISCONSIN'S ALUMINUM COOKWARE

## Worth the Extra Penny?

In some cases, cooking up a historical recipe involves more than just using the right ingredients; the tools and kitchen utensils of the time are often equally important to the re-creation of a dish. The modern muffin pan—used for dishes such as breakfast puffs—is likely very similar to what home bakers would have used when the following recipe was first published in 1914. Most historical kitchens included items made of tin, aluminum, and cast iron, and in Wisconsin, aluminum cookware became especially popular after the turn of the century. Wisconsin was at one point home to the largest aluminum cookware manufacturing operation in the world.[1]

**A 1925 advertisement for Mirro brand aluminum ware.** *Eagle River Review*, June 11, 1925

As the twentieth century approached, struggling communities in northern Wisconsin, bereft of logging companies, needed new industries to support their residents. The town of Two Rivers was so eager, in fact, that it lent two thousand dollars to the Aluminum Manufacturing Company, a brand-new business founded by Joseph Koenig. The money came with a stipulation: the growing company was to remain in Two Rivers.[2] In 1909, Koenig's company entered a three-way merger with Henry Vits's Manitowoc Aluminum Novelty Company and the New Jersey Aluminum Company of Newark to form the Aluminum Goods Manufacturing Company. The headquarters of the new entity was in neighboring Manitowoc, although factories remained in Two Rivers and other locations.

Soon, plans to revolutionize the US cookware scene were forged. In 1917, the company, locally known as the Goods, launched the high-end cookware brand Mirro.[3] Comparing the brand's products to alternatives at the time, we may safely assume that many consumers initially experienced sticker shock. A Mirro kettle in 1922 cost $3.80 (roughly $65 today), while an enamelware kettle with a tin lid cost as little as 25¢ (roughly $4).[4] Despite this disparity, the Aluminum Goods Manufacturing Company believed it could market its brand of aluminum as worth the price based on the material's "resistance to corrosion, high conductivity to heat, good appearance, resistance to chipping or cracking, and ease of cleaning."[5] To promote this high quality material, the Goods ran an effective marketing campaign, including in-person demonstrations around the state. Consumers were convinced, and by 1920, the Goods had become a $12 million corporation.[6] Hence, it's likely that much of the aluminum cookware used by Wisconsin newspaper readers came directly from the Badger State.

# Breakfast Puffs

*Vernon County Censor*, October 28, 1914[7]

Makes 6 puffs

2 eggs

1 cup milk

1 teaspoon butter, melted

1 ½ cups flour

2 teaspoons baking powder

½ teaspoon salt

**Breakfast Puffs.**

Two eggs, one cupful milk, 1½ cupfuls flour, one-half teaspoonful salt, one teaspoonful melted butter, two teaspoonfuls baking powder. Beat the the eggs very thoroughly and add the milk and butter. Sift flour, salt and baking powder twice, add the liquid ingredients and beat two minutes. Pour into hot, well-greased muffin pans and bake 20 minutes in a hot oven.

## Optional Variations

**BACON CHEESE SCALLION**

3 strips of crispy bacon

½ cup shredded sharp cheddar

1 scallion, finely chopped

**ROSEMARY CHEDDAR**

¾ teaspoon fresh chopped rosemary

¼ cup shredded sharp cheddar

**CINNAMON SUGAR**

1 tablespoon butter

1 tablespoon brown sugar

1 teaspoon cinnamon

Preheat oven to 425°F. In a medium bowl, beat eggs thoroughly. Add milk and melted butter and mix well to combine.

In a separate larger bowl, sift together flour, baking powder, and salt. Add the liquid ingredients, and beat well for approximately 2 minutes.

Pour mixture into a well-greased muffin pan and bake until fully cooked, about 20 minutes.

Variations: For the bacon cheese scallion and rosemary cheddar variations, add the additional ingredients to the liquid ingredients after beating. For the cinnamon sugar variety, mix melted butter, brown sugar, and cinnamon together in a separate bowl. Swirl dollops of the mixture into the batter after it has been poured into the muffin pan, then bake.

# WILD RICE

## A Native Culinary Tradition

Nowadays, rice is widely available in an array of shapes, sizes, and colors. Before the establishment of modern rice cultivation and trade, however, people had much more limited options. In fact, for most of human history, the land we now call Wisconsin provided just one variety—and technically it isn't even rice. *Zizania aquatica*, an acquatic grass commonly referred to as wild rice, is native to Wisconsin and has historically been an important crop for local American Indian nations like the Ojibwe and Menominee. According to Thomas Pecore Weso in his book *Good Seeds*, "*meno* is the Menominee word for good, and *min* is grain, seed, or berry, so the word means 'good grain' or 'good seed.' The Menominee Tribe of Wisconsin is named for this—*ee* means people, so we are the Wild Rice People."[1] The crop is an essential component of the Menominee diet, complementing protein consumed in the form of fish and game. Over centuries, the Native populations who settled in the Great Lakes region of the United States and Canada developed and perfected techniques to harvest the grains of these tall stalks, which grow in shallow bodies of water, by knocking the mature grains into their canoes.[2]

Early Indigenous peoples would begin their harvests in early fall, and they would work for a couple weeks or at least until they had collected enough wild rice to provide for the community during the coming winter. After Euro-American settlement, when the harvest was good, some Indigenous communities would sell their surplus to the newcomers. When the crop failed, as it did in 1867 in the Chippewa Falls region, communities suffered severely because of their reliance on wild rice to survive the

**An Ojibwa woman, Francis Mike, harvesting wild rice on Totogatic Lake sometime before 1960.** WHI IMAGE ID 24509

winter. As the *Prescott Journal* reported in January of 1868, "The *Union and Times*, of Chippewa Falls, says that the Indians of that region must suffer greatly, and in many instances starve, this winter. The cause of this destitution is owing to the failure of the wild rice crop."[3] Many European immigrants who settled in Wisconsin grew to like the grain, and they sometimes called it "mock oats"—a name that probably derived from the way they saw it being processed and served.[4] In 1841, the *Southport Telegraph* praised the taste and versatility of wild rice, suggesting that readers use the long, starchy seeds instead of white rice in puddings or soups.[5]

In contrast to its white counterpart, wild rice was not cultivated commercially for a long time.[6] In the early twentieth century, some non-Native communities around the state started to sow the grain—but not for human consumption. The goal was to attract ducks and the hunters that the rice planters hoped would follow.[7] Today, some Native communities still harvest wild rice in the traditional ways, and it is also farmed commercially in the Midwest and beyond, allowing people to prepare it the way the local American Indian nations have for millennia and to find new ways to incorporate it into modern cuisine. If you are an oatmeal aficionado looking for a change, a breakfast of wild rice may be just the historical twist on the meal that you have been seeking.

**This image of wild rice growing in shallow water appeared in a 1922 USDA article, "Wild Rice Good for Human Food."** *Iowa County Democrat,* October 12, 1922

# Breakfast Rice

*Iron County News*, March 14, 1914[8]

Makes 4 servings

1 cup water

1 ¾ cups milk

1 cup rice (wild rice works well)

Pinch salt

Pinch nutmeg, if desired

Splash cream, if desired

Fresh fruit and nuts of your choice, if desired

> Boiled rice, boiled well until it is light and flaky, eaten with thick cream and a bit of nutmeg, can well be the staple dish at breakfast for grown-up or child. The fats in the cream supplement the good qualities of the rice in just the right manner.

Rinse rice. In a medium pot, bring to boil milk, water, rice, and salt. Cover and let simmer on medium heat until liquid has been absorbed, about 45 minutes for wild rice.

Add nutmeg and cream and top with fruit and nuts, if desired.

# 5

# EATING IN
# A FRESH-AIR FASHION

## Camping and Cooking

In August 1911, three friends, Edward, Ernest, and Fred, launched their rowboat into the Wisconsin River near their hometown of Portage.[1] They had packed overnight camping gear and cooking utensils to embark on a journey that, according to the *Portage Register*, no one had navigated for a considerable time.[2] It was an exciting adventure for the three young men who planned to follow the Wisconsin River down to where it met the Baraboo River, which they then intended to navigate all the way to Baraboo before returning back home the way they had come. They were not the only ones seeking a river camping adventure that summer. For Portage youth, traveling down the Wisconsin River and camping was becoming a popular activity.

While today many of us think of setting up camp as a fun way to spend a summer weekend, the word *camp* has meant different things to different people throughout history. There have been military camps, for example, and other occupational camps for laborers, such as those in the logging industry in northern Wisconsin. And by necessity, camping continues to be a way that unhoused populations and refugees create shelter. By contrast, camping as a leisure activity with the purpose of enjoying nature has almost always required the means to acquire gear and the luxury of free time and travel. For many years, this type of camping was attainable only by the wealthy, who had figured out ways to spend time outdoors without sacrificing too many of the

**This 1915 cartoon pokes fun at the turn-of-the-century camping craze.**
*Eagle River Review*, November 5, 1915

comforts of their homes. Today, a luxurious camping experience is sometimes referred to as "glamping," but this form of camping is anything but new.

William Henry Harrison Murray is often credited with starting the first recreational camping craze in the United States with his 1869 book *Adventures in the Wilderness*. Inspired by the publication, a wave of well-to-do campers followed his lead. Critics, however, bewailed the lack of minimalism in his approach. As a reporter for the *Watertown Weekly Republican* argued: "There are many ways in which the camp may be made comfortable for the seekers for health and change who cannot indulge themselves in the luxuries of those Adirondack campers who supply their rustic dwellings with brass beds and porcelain tubs. That sort of thing is not camping at all, in the real sense of the word."[3] Over time, recreational camping did indeed become simpler—and, therefore, more attainable. A growing number of campers avoided the logistical hassle of bringing along luxury furnishings such as beds. The automobile proved to be a game changer by further mobilizing people, and it also paved the way for motorized camping vehicles. In the 1910s, several Wisconsin newspapers began publishing syndicated columns by Albert Neely Hall and Dorothy Perkins on backyard camping with children as a way of preparing them for camping in the wild.

By 1920, northern Wisconsin had become a popular camping destination for in-state tourists, as well as travelers from Illinois, Indiana, and Ohio. After the state began experiencing a boom in tourism, politicians such as Chairman John Adam Hazelwood of the Wisconsin Highway Commission called for all cities in the northern part of the state swarming with summer tourists to build additional campgrounds.[4]

While spending time outdoors seems to have been on many people's minds in the early twentieth century, few written accounts of this early recreational camping provide a glimpse into how the logistics of cooking were handled. Writer Christine Terhune Herrick, an avid advocate of simplified camping, suggested the use of practical but aesthetic cookware in 1904: "The best camp outfit, both for the stove and the table, is of the blue and white enamel iron ware, which is light and durable and not unpleasing to look at. Stone china is ugly as well as heavy and anything finer or more fragile is out of the question."[5]

We don't know if the three young men from Portage followed Herrick's advice as they packed their "complete cooking and sleeping outfits" into their boat in 1911.[6] They may have cooked their meals in enamelware over a fire, or they may have opted for even more minimalist recipes requiring no cookware at all, such as Fire-Baked Eggs or Fish Kebabs (see "Mr. Smith Went Fishing Last Saturday" on page 122), that could be found in newspapers that year.

# Fire-Baked Eggs

*Wausau Pilot,* October 3, 1911[7]

Makes 4 servings

> Baked Eggs—Make a small hole in the top to prevent bursting and stand in rows against hot stones around the camp fire.

4 eggs

Using an egg piercer or corkscrew, make a small hole in the bottom of the raw eggs to prevent them from bursting.

Stand the eggs in rows against hot stones around the campfire. Cook for about 45 minutes.

Note: Unfortunately, there is no way of telling when the eggs are fully cooked until one is removed from the fire and opened. To make sure everyone gets an egg, err on the side of caution and cook more than needed.

Do not move the eggs closer to the fire to speed up the cooking process. They may explode, causing you to spend a significant amount of time removing shell debris and raw egg from your hair.

# SALADS AND DRESSINGS

# 6

# ALL IN THE NAME
# OF HEALTH

## Historical Nutrition Advice

An analysis of historical foods would not be complete without addressing the evolution of nutrition advice. Although nutrition science is still a rather young field of study—the first vitamin was "isolated and chemically defined" in 1926—people have been dispensing nutrition advice for centuries.[2] In addition to, and often alongside, recipes, Wisconsin newspapers recorded a vast amount of early information, ideas, and recommendations about nutrition. The advice came from official government sources—the US Department of Agriculture's first published work on dietary advice came out in 1894—as well as the food industry and agricultural stakeholders.[3] Some recommendations made in this time period, when vitamins were just being discovered and the nutritional value of different foods was just beginning to be understood, now seem outdated. However, a number of claims made by nutrition professionals from this era will sound familiar to the contemporary consumer. Unsurprisingly, there has always been a fine line between the communication of scientific discoveries and the promotion of products.

Some nutrition advice was published out of a legitimate concern for the health of the population. During the early twentieth century, malnourishment was especially prevalent in poor urban communities. As a result, public and private charitable organizations launched educational campaigns in news publications to help readers understand the importance of a balanced diet. In 1924, the *Vilas County News* printed "a dozen good health rules for children," created by the New York Association for Improving the Condition of the Poor, illustrating some of the accepted ideas and recommendations of the time.

**Emphatically do:**

1. Use milk—fresh, clean, whole milk for children. Every growing child should have a quart a day in some form.
2. Eat plenty of vegetables.
3. Be sure that a school child has a good luncheon, not candy, pickles, and ice cream cones.
4. Eat coarse food, such as oatmeal, bran muffins and vegetables, so that the bowels will not be constipated.

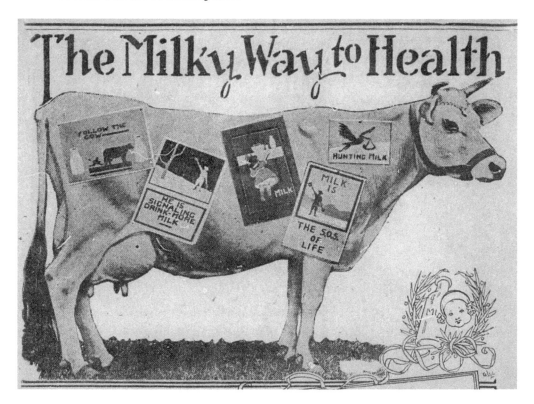

**An image from a 1920 USDA milk campaign.** *Wauwatosa News,* October 8, 1920

5. Eat slowly and chew food well.

6. Have the meals at the same hours each day.

7. Eat only bread, or crackers and milk, or bread and butter between meals, and only in the middle of the morning or afternoon.

8. Wash hands and face before eating.

9. Drink plenty of water between meals.

10. Be in bed by 9 o'clock or before.

11. Have windows open in the sleeping room at night.

12. Brush the teeth at least once a day.

**Important DON'TS:**

Do not let the children eat pork or veal, much meat of any kind, fried foods, rich pies and cakes, strong spice and vinegar, green or spoiled fruit.

Do not let children drink tea, coffee, beer, wine, sodas.

Do not let them eat between meals, except the things named in No. 7 above. Do not let them eat candy, ice cream cones, nuts, cakes and cookies between meals.[4]

On the other hand, some nutrition advice was distributed in the form of advertisements from food and drug companies. Aimed at selling a product rather than solving a public health problem, these ads regularly made fictitious claims, promoted pseudoscience, and attempted to capitalize on the average consumer's limited understanding of nutrition.

"Nervousness is a question of nutrition," asserted one such ad from 1899. "Food for the nerves is what you need to put you right, and the best nerve food in the world is Dr. Williams' Pink Pills for Pale People."[5] One 1903 ad using pseudoscientific language insisted, "Doctor Pierce's Golden Medical Discovery cures diseases of the stomach and other organs of digestion and nutrition. It strengthens the body in the only way possible, by enabling the assimilation of the nutrition extracted from food."[6] "Mother's Oats are the best food," another ad confidently claimed. "They contain more nutrition than the same bulk of almost anything else people eat. You can put more sound flesh on your bones—you can put more life and vitality in your marrow—you can put a riper, richer, clearer blood in your veins and more endurance in your brain on a diet of Mother's Oats than you can with any other food that has ever been found."[7] It wasn't until 1906, when the Pure Food and Drug Act was passed, that false and misleading nutrition and medical claims like these were regulated (see "A Vindication of the Prune" on page 146).

The agricultural industry also published nutrition advice in Wisconsin's newspapers, usually aiming to garner demand for whatever products it was promoting. Some articles made a case for the product's nutritional superiority or its role in a well-balanced diet. In Wisconsin, the dairy industry has been especially active, circulating campaigns about the nutritional advantages of milk over beef and stressing the importance of milk in childhood development. The *Northern Wisconsin Advertiser*, for example, published an article in 1922 sponsored by the College of Agriculture at the University of Wisconsin and the Dairy Division of the US Department of Agriculture that read, in part: "Milk is the indispensable food for children, and . . . whole milk in some form must be furnished [to] them if the nutrition of the average child is to be maintained and if normal growth in height and weight is to be assured. Lowered nutrition in children means decreased vitality and lowered resistance to disease. If the nutrition of our children is impaired for any length of time, full juvenile development will be permanently arrested."[8]

Although campaigns like these could be somewhat aggressive in tone, they proved to be incredibly effective, as the *Washburn Times* noted in 1921: "Cities having an aggregate population of over 5,000,000 have had milk campaigns lasting from one to two weeks. Careful reports show that these cities have increased their milk consumption about 16 per cent since the beginning of the campaigns."[9]

Nutrition advice also found its way into recipes of the time. With a name that highlights its then-modern health consciousness, the Twentieth Century Salad, for example, blends a mix of fruit, vegetables, nuts, and dairy to create a dish that likely appealed to turn-of-the-century diners attuned to ingredients' nutritional values. If there is one thing we can learn from historical nutrition advice, it is to approach claims with a discerning eye and an appropriate amount of skepticism. What is recommended to facilitate health today may be rendered obsolete tomorrow.

# Twentieth Century Salad

*Watertown Leader*, August 4, 1911[10]

Makes 12 servings

## Dressing

12 egg yolks

1 cup butter, melted

1 cup white vinegar

Juice of 2 lemons (about 6 tablespoons)

1 tablespoon sugar

1 teaspoon salt

Pinch paprika

1 cup heavy whipping cream

## Salad

6 oranges

½ pound white or green grapes

½ pound pecan halves

4 cups chopped celery

Twentieth Century Salad—Take six oranges, peel cover and seed them, and cut the fruit in small pieces with a sharp scissors. Skin and seed one-half pound of white grapes and mix the fruit with one-half pound of pecan nuts and one quart of chopped celery. Mix all these ingredients well and stir in a dressing made the following way: Beat well the yolks of twelve eggs, put in an earthen bowl over a pot of hot water and stir them. After the eggs have become warm add one cupful of melted butter and one-half pint of vinegar, which may be weakened with a little warm water if too sharp. Stir the dressing until it is perfectly smooth, being careful not to let it cook too long or it will curdle. Give it time to become perfectly cold. Then add the juice of two lemons, one tablespoonful of sugar, one teaspoonful of salt, and a pinch of paprika or red pepper. Whip one-half pint of double cream and stir it in; then put away for several hours.

With the above quantities there should be enough salad for twelve persons and is nice for a company luncheon at a moderate cost.

For dressing: Beat egg yolks in a bowl over a hot pot of water or in a double boiler. When the yolks are warm, add butter and vinegar, which may be weakened with a little warm water if its taste is too sharp. Stir the dressing until it is smooth, being careful to prevent curdling by not letting it overcook. Let the mixture cool, then add lemon juice, sugar, salt, and paprika. Whip cream and stir it in. Refrigerate for several hours.

For salad: Peel oranges, seed them, and cut them into ½-inch pieces. Cut grapes and remove seeds, if necessary. (Note: The original recipe also calls for the grapes to be skinned. Many modern varieties of grapes do not have very thick skin, allowing you to skip this tedious task.) Mix the fruit with pecans and celery.

Pour the cooled dressing over the salad mixture, mix, and serve.

# LANDRETH'S LEGACY

## Commercial Canning in Wisconsin

Wisconsin has played an important part in US agricultural history—it is called the Dairy State, after all. The birthplace of the Babcock test, used to determine the fat content in milk, and the nation's frequent leader in cranberry production was also home to the earliest commercial canning operation west of the Appalachian Mountains.[1] In fact, by the twentieth century, Wisconsin was leading the nation in commercial vegetable processing.

It all began with seed farmer Albert Landreth. Born in Pennsylvania, Landreth came from a family with a long history in seed production and sales. His family's business—the David Landreth Seed Company, which had been in operation since 1784—sent him to Manitowoc, Wisconsin, in 1875 to manage the company's local seed pea production. However, Landreth was a skilled businessman with a vision, and soon after his arrival, he founded his own company—the Albert Landreth Seed Company, which still exists today as Lakeside Foods.

**Albert Landreth**

WILL SELL

**Reliable Garden Seeds**

DURING THE

SEASON OF 1884

At his Warehouse on Buffalo St.

MANITOWOC.

CAUTION.—We have no connection with the Philadelphia house of Landreth & Sons

**An ad for the Albert Landreth Seed Company prior to the launch of the company's canning business.** *Manitowoc Pilot,* January 17, 1884

The new business made its food preservation debut in 1889 when Landreth start-ed to further commodify his pea seed business by commercially canning his crops for distribution.[2] The process was no easy feat. Landreth's first batches of canned peas were, according to a history of the company published in 1987, "done by hand, with-out the assistance of electrical power. Cans and lids were hammered into shape, as-sembled and soldered together. Cans were filled through a small hole in the top of the can, and a tin cap was soldered over the hole prior to the product being cooked."[3] The company was the first, and went on to become the most prolific, operation of its kind, turning its owner into a nationally known entrepreneur.[4]

A key component in Landreth's entrepreneurial success was his utilization, or some might say takeover, of the local newspaper for extensive self-promotion. Landreth placed ads for his seed company in nearly every issue of the *Manitowoc Pilot*; he regularly managed to get upward of four advertisements to appear on a single page. The *Pilot* itself couldn't help but attest that Landreth "understands how to advertise. He drops into a newspaper office when he has work of this kind on hand, moves to suspend the rules and that all regular business be declared off for the time.... He then proceeds to run the office about as he pleases until he gets such notices inserted that he wants."[5] Though he may have had a heavy hand when working with the local press, Landreth's relationship with the *Pilot* was mutually beneficial. The paper published these laudatory words in 1885: "Albert Landreth is going to make the heart of the printer glad with fruit. He likes a printer, and nothing does him more good than to make one of 'em feel good."[6]

By 1893, Landreth's canning operation employed around six hundred individuals and was leading the nation in pea canning production.[7] The success of Landreth's pioneering venture became a catalyst for Wisconsin's burgeoning vegetable process-ing industry. A history of the state's canning industry published in 2019 claimed Wisconsin "was packing half of the nation's total crop of canning vegetables" by 1920.[8] In addition to peas, vegetables such as beets, sweet corn, cucumbers, and snap beans also began to be commercially processed in the state. By 1931, Wisconsin's commercial canning business was at its peak, with 170 canneries in operation.[9] The new abun-dance and convenience of shelf-stable produce allowed home cooks to whip up dishes like Hungarian Salad even if they didn't have fresh beets or a cucumber handy.

# Hungarian Salad

*Odanah Star*, August 16, 1912[10]

Makes 4 servings

1 cup potatoes, boiled

1 beet, cooked

1 small cucumber

3–4 ounces watercress

1 (3- or 4-ounce) can sardines, drained

4 tablespoons olive oil

2 tablespoons vinegar

1 teaspoon salt

1 teaspoon paprika

> Hungarian Salad.—One cupful of cold boiled potatoes sliced thin, one cold beet cut in small pieces, one small cucumber sliced, four sardines, four tablespoonfuls of olive oil, two tablespoonfuls of vinegar, one teaspoonful of salt and one of paprika.
>
> Mix well the vegetables salt and paprika; add the sardines from which the bones are removed. Mix in the oil with a silver or wooden fork, turning it over gently so as not to break the vegetables. Add the vinegar in the same way. Serve on watercress.

Slice potatoes, beet, and cucumber. Place slices on a bed of watercress and add sardines.

For the dressing, mix oil, vinegar, salt, and paprika and drizzle on top of the salad.

# 8
# NELLIE MAXWELL

## A Rural Star in the Kitchen

In the early years of Wisconsin's local press, after the state's first newspaper was published in 1833, newspapers often served quite small communities. All that was needed to publish a newspaper was someone to write it and someone with access to a printing press. Occasionally, they were one and the same person. Toward the turn of the twentieth century, however, things began to change. As the printing industry made technological advances and information started to spread more quickly, the news became more homogenous. Syndicate agencies sold newspapers the right to print advice columns, entertainment sections, and comic strips, among other things. Small publications utilized this service to offer popular content that they could not afford to produce in-house. As the service became more popular, the same syndicated content began to appear in newspapers across the nation.

Rather than reflecting Wisconsin's regional cuisine and locally available ingredients, syndicated recipes were more likely to

An undated portrait of Nellie Maxwell during her time as a Wisconsin Farmers' Institute instructor. WHI IMAGE ID 59353

Nellie Maxwell's syndicated column, The Kitchen Cabinet, appeared in newspapers across the nation in the early 1900s.

feature trends and dishes from other parts of the country—to the chagrin of many rural Wisconsinites. That is, until a cooking column authored by Wisconsin-based Nellie Maxwell entered the scene. As a reporter from Ely, Minnesota, explained in 1930, "One reason why [Maxwell's] recipes and her practical advice on household matters are so popular with [rural readers] is because she understands so thoroughly their problems and their resources. That is because she was born and reared in a rural community, and it was upon a foundation of first-hand practical knowledge of the life of a woman on the farm and in the small town that she built her college education in domestic science."[1]

Originally from Neenah, where she was born in 1867, Maxwell went on to study education at the University of Wisconsin.[2] After teaching at public schools, she enrolled in Milwaukee-Downer College to study household economics.[3] She was able to combine both of her fields of study when she moved out of state to teach at farmers' institutes affiliated with the state agricultural colleges of Iowa and Nebraska. Her students, who were mostly farm women, learned about efficiency in the kitchen and ways of "taking much of the drudgery out of their work."[4] After a few years, Maxwell returned to Wisconsin, where she began to offer similar lectures and demonstrations across the state in conjunction with her alma mater, the University of Wisconsin.

It was back in her home state where she successfully expanded her career beyond instruction and became a well-known household and kitchen writer. She began writing pieces for university publications and a bulletin for Wisconsin farm women. In 1909, articles she authored began appearing in various publications around the country, featuring recipes and tips such as how to make the "Perfect Jelly," the benefits of consuming rhubarb, and the following recipe for cabbage salad.[5] Through these pieces, she established herself as a trusted expert and soon started her own column, The Kitchen Cabinet, which she wrote for a New York syndicate. It was published well into the 1930s. The column appeared not only in the Midwest but as far west as Washington State, as far east as Vermont, and as far south as Louisiana. Maxwell died in 1936 in Antigo. Although her work influenced countless American kitchens, she never received appropriate recognition—even her obituary only briefly mentioned her writing career.[6]

# Cabbage Salad

*Ladysmith News-Budget,* July 16, 1915[7]

Makes 12 servings

1 head white cabbage, finely shredded

1 head purple cabbage, finely shredded

1 cup sour cream

2 tablespoons sugar

2 teaspoons salt

2 tablespoons white vinegar, adjusted
   to taste

> **Cabbage Salad.**— Shred cabbage very fine and plunge into cold water to crisp. Drain and dress with sour cream, sugar, salt and if not quite sour enough a very little vinegar may be added. This is a salad which can be enjoyed at any meal with almost any combination of foods.

Plunge shredded cabbage into cold water to crisp, then drain.

In a medium bowl, mix sour cream, sugar, salt, and vinegar. Dress cabbage with the mixture.

# 9

# WISCONSIN GOES BANANAS

## A Short History of a Long Berry's Arrival in the Midwest

A banana in Wisconsin is a long way from home, and considering how fast they turn brown in contemporary kitchens, it's easy to see why the history of the banana in the American Midwest does not go as far back as it does in more tropical parts of the planet. Bananas began to appear in Wisconsin newspapers in the middle of the nineteenth century. In the 1860s, the local press printed excerpts describing the fruit—or, more specifically, berry—written by Alexander von Humboldt (1769–1859). The German geographer, explorer, and naturalist praised the nutritional and agricultural value of the banana, doubting "whether there is any plant on the globe which, [in so] small a space of ground, can produce as great a mass of nutriment. . . . The produce of the banana to that of wheat is one hundred and thirty-three to one, and to that of potatoes as forty-four to one.' "[1]

Bananas also started appearing in newspaper correspondences from Brazil, Mexico, and even Florida, where farmers were experimenting with growing the plant on US soil. Because most bananas continued to have a long travel route to the United States, however, they were most common in port cities on the coasts. In these areas, the drastically rising rate of banana consumption caused a serious problem. Many banana lovers disposed of the peel by simply throwing it on the ground, causing others to slip, fall, suffer severe injuries, or—in the case of Thomas Hughes, a forty-two-year-old contractor from Syracuse, New York—even die.[2] As a result, many people called for banana peel disposal regulations, and some states even instituted them. While the occurrence was not as common in the Midwest, some Wisconsinites were

In this 1928 photo, the A & P at 1355 Williamson Street in Madison boasted an impressive window display of bananas. WHI IMAGE ID 21754

also harmed by banana peels. In Racine in 1901, for example, a Mr. H. Stone slipped, broke his ankle, and suffered internal injuries.[3] Eventually, slipping on a banana peel became a trope in the humor and entertainment columns rather than the local incident reports.

Although advertisements for bananas in Wisconsin grocery stores didn't appear in newspapers until the late 1870s, the fruit was not completely foreign to Wisconsinites, as it was mentioned more or less casually in other contexts. The *Kenosha Telegraph* reported the arrival of a tropical fruit shipment including pineapples and bananas in 1871, and the *Wood County Reporter* ran a recipe for dressed bananas in 1874.[4] It suggested serving them "dressed with sugar dissolved in water," while other papers recommended making the fruit more digestible by cooking it first. This guidance raises the question of whether the product used was what we now call plantains, rather than bananas.

The variety commonly available in contemporary supermarkets is the Cavendish banana, which was cultivated in England and then introduced to Central American plantations. It has been a poster child for American imperialism since the 1950s. However, prior to the rise of the Cavendish, Wisconsinites likely got to taste different varieties including red bananas, advertised in the *Grant County Herald* in 1912.[5] For this reason, getting a true taste of the past using this ingredient could be tricky—unless you can find an heirloom banana.

# Banana Salad

*Mineral Point Tribune,* December 14, 1916[6]

Makes 4 servings

1 head lettuce (butterhead works well)

4 bananas

¼ cup mayonnaise (see Mayonnaise
   recipe on page 57)

¼ cup peanuts, chopped

> Banana Salad—Cut bananas in halves crosswise and lay on lettuce or by themselves on a flat dish. Sprinkle well with chopped peanuts and serve with mayonnaise dressing.

On individual plates, arrange beds of lettuce leaves. Cut bananas in half crosswise and lay across lettuce.

Dress with mayonnaise and sprinkle well with chopped peanuts.

# 10
# THE CHERRY ON TOP

### The Americanization of a European Garnish

Maraschino cherries are an integral part of American cocktail and dessert culture. Not only can the bright red fruit be found swimming in a Wisconsin favorite, the Old Fashioned, but it is also, literally, the cherry on top of many sundaes. Maraschino cherries have a long history that can be traced back to Croatia. However, the fruit that we now know as a maraschino cherry is, in many ways, a product of US Prohibition.

Originally, the maraschino cherry was a special variety of wild sour cherry, the marasca cherry, preserved in maraschino liqueur, which is also made from the fruit. Europeans were quite fond of this delicacy and did not want to do without it when they settled in the United States. Since the import was expensive, they soon looked for cheaper alternatives. Clever cherry lovers began experimenting with locally grown cherries, such as the Royal Ann variety, that could be preserved in alcohol, almond oil, sugar, and dye. Some newspapers even published recipes for making maraschino cherries at home.[1] Despite their significant deviations from the original European product, the US versions of the beloved garnish that hit the market were also advertised as maraschino cherries. Consumers likely welcomed the item's sudden affordability, but most were probably unaware of the difference between the original and the new, low-cost product.

In the early twentieth century, the US Department of Agriculture got involved. In the interest of consumer protection, the government agency that would later come to be known as the Food and Drug Administration took a closer look at the fruity garnish and the legitimacy of the products being made in the United States.

The maraschino cherry was just one of many products of interest to the agency at the time. The Pure Food and Drug Act of 1906 was the first of a series of consumer protection laws beginning to regulate adulteration in consumer products. Not all maraschino cherry consumers were happy about the investigations, though. In 1906, the *Manitowoc Pilot* printed the headline "Adieu to Maraschino: Festive Cherry Must Abandon the Punch Bowl" to accompany an article about a professor who addressed the pure food legislation: "He playfully expressed regret that, as a result of the recent pure food legislation, the people of Wisconsin will lose the Marischino [*sic*] cherry from the punch bowl."[2] Despite consumer protest, however, 1912 Food Inspection Decision 141 ruled that the label "maraschino cherries" must be used exclusively for marasca cherries in maraschino liqueur. Anything else needed to be labeled as "imitation maraschino cherries."[3]

This, of course, did not mean that the imitations disappeared, as predicted by the professor and the *Manitowoc Pilot* six years prior. In fact, Prohibition, which went into effect in 1920, provided new motivation for people to continue experimenting with the preserved cherry. While the demand for maraschino cherries as ingredients in alcoholic beverages declined, their consumption and popularity as a confectionary and food garnish continued, and people suddenly needed a legal nonalcoholic imitation. In the late 1920s, the American maraschino cherry we find in grocery stores today was developed at Oregon State University.[4] It had to be labeled as an imitation at the time. But by 1939, the US Food and Drug Administration was finally convinced that the general US population associated the name *maraschino* with the imitation cherry rather than the original. For the first time in over two decades, the label "maraschino cherry" could be used freely once again.[5]

The complex history of the maraschino cherry presents historical recipe lovers with a conundrum. When a recipe calls for maraschino cherries, it is impossible to know whether home cooks used the American imitation, knowingly or not, or the original. Although the original can be found at some specialty food stores today, recipes in this book have been tested using the imitation—not only in the interest of home economics but also to get a taste of the American inventive spirit.

# Grapefruit and Maraschino Cherry Salad

*Northern Wisconsin Advertiser*, December 16, 1910[6]

Makes 4 servings

1 grapefruit

1 (10-ounce) jar of maraschino cherries, drained

1 cup French dressing (see French Dressing recipe on page 52)

8–12 ounces lettuce (spring mix works well)

½ cup mayonnaise (see Mayonnaise recipe on page 57), if desired

A very pretty and also delicious salad may be made using grape fruit and marischino cherries. Arrange head lettuce leaves in nests and on these a mixture of grape fruit in small pieces with a few of the red cherries. The fruit should be marinated in French dressing before serving. A teaspoonful of mayonnaise may be added if desired.

Peel and skin grapefruit and cut into bite-size pieces.

Marinate grapefruit and maraschino cherries in French dressing for about 10 minutes. Don't marinate for too long or the grapefruit pieces will fall apart.

Arrange lettuce leaves into nests, and place marinated fruit on top.

Serve with mayonnaise on the side, if desired.

# 11

# MEASUREMENTS AND STANDARDIZATION

## A Tale of Culinary Frustration

When cooking with historical recipes, it's quite common to come across outdated measurements such as a dram of mace or, in the case of this chapter's recipe, a light saltspoon of cayenne pepper. These antiquated measurements can cause frustration as they need to be converted to units used in contemporary kitchens, thus adding an additional step to the cooking process. Moreover, getting the conversions wrong can ruin a whole recipe. Especially in baking, correct measurements are vital to achieving intended outcomes, like the perfect cake.

In her 1896 book, cooking expert and Boston Cooking School principal Fannie Merritt Farmer emphasized the importance of standardized measurements, writing, "Correct measurements are absolutely necessary to insure [sic] the best results."[1] In 1898, the *Eagle River Review* published a list of measuring "facts" to help readers understand different units depending on

**Facts in Cooking.**

A heaped spoonful is all the spoon will hold.

All dry materials should be sifted before measuring.

A cup holding just half a pint is the standard measuring cup.

A teaspoonful of salt, pepper and spice is a level teaspoonful.

A teaspoonful of flour, sugar or butter is a rounded tablespoonful.

Half a spoonful is measured by dividing through the middle lengthwise..

A cupful is all the cup will hold without running over—full to the brim.

A scant cupful is within a fourth of an inch of the top.

**These tips on how to make sense of measurements were published in the Household Department section of the *Eagle River Review* in 1898.** *Eagle River Review, May 5, 1898*

the substance being measured.[2] Still, even decades later, some recipes continued to call for difficult-to-estimate units, such as "two large cups of evaporated apples."[3] Other recipes relied on what may have been a relatively standard packaging unit, like "one and one-half squares of unsweetened chocolate," not anticipating that manufacturers would produce squares of different sizes in the future, rendering many recipes confusing at best or, at worst, completely useless.[4]

The US Constitution grants Congress the power to "fix the Standard of Weights and Measures," and while this power was utilized to standardize measurements for trade, the realm of the kitchen remained mostly untouched for almost a century.[5] It was not until the rise of home economists in the second half of the nineteenth century that things began to change. As the general population became aware that running a household involved science and that the knowledge of said science increased efficiency and safety, home economics became a gateway through which many women entered into higher education and the sciences. In 1923, the Bureau of Home Economics was founded under the US Department of Agriculture, and its staff began studying and promoting cooking methods, food storage, and standardized kitchen equipment such as measuring cups.[6] There was even a push for the adoption of the metric system, a success story that has yet to be written.

To make this cookbook more accessible, we have converted all measurements to the current US standard, even if it may be subject to change in the next century or so.

**This patented Hawkes French Dressing Mixing Bottle was sold at J. B. Donovan & Co. in Baraboo in 1916.** *Baraboo Weekly News*, January 6, 1916

# French Dressing

*Northern Wisconsin Advertiser,* August 8, 1907[7]

Makes approximately 1 quart

2 medium shallots, finely chopped

1 tablespoon finely chopped fresh parsley

1 tablespoon finely chopped fresh chives,

1 clove garlic, finely crushed

4 teaspoons salt

1 teaspoon white pepper

1 teaspoon curry powder

½ teaspoon Dijon mustard

¼ teaspoon ground mustard seeds

¼ teaspoon cayenne pepper

Zest of 1 lemon, freshly grated

2 ¾ cups olive oil, divided

1 ½ cups white wine vinegar, divided

Mix together shallots, herbs, spices, mustard, and lemon zest, then add 1 tablespoon of olive oil and mash until this mixture is a pulp.

Gradually add 4 tablespoons of vinegar and mix thoroughly again. Finally, add remaining oil and vinegar.

Transfer to a jar with a lid and refrigerate. When ready to serve, shake well and strain the mixture. Pour over salad.

## SALAD FOR THE SUMMER.

### French Dressing a Requisite, and Easy to Make.

The first requisite of a delicious summer salad is French dressing. Boiled dressings or mayonnaise are rather heavy to combine with fresh vegetables.

The real French dressing sounds like a complicated article, but it can be made in qualities, poured into a covered jar and kept on ice indefinitely. Its flavor is truly delicious and far above the insipid mixture of oil and vinegar which generally passes under the title of "French dressing."

In a deep china bowl place a level teaspoon of oriental curry powder, half a teaspoon of French mustard, a light saltspoon of English ground mustard, a light saltspoon of cayenne pepper, one teaspoon of parsley, fresh, finely chopped, washed and drained, half a teaspoon finely chopped fresh chives two medium shallots, pelled and chopped, one-fourth of a small bean of garlic, finely crushed, four teaspoons of salt, and one light teaspoon of white pepper, the rind of a lemon, finely chopped. Mix these ingredients together firmly with a silver or wooden fork, and then add a tablespoon of olive oil that has been chilled, and mash until this mixture is a pulp. Add gradually four tablespoons of good white wine vinegar, mix thoroughly again and add more vinegar and oil in the proportion of two-thirds oil to one-third vinegar, until you have a quart in all. Press through a fine strainer into a stone or glass jar and set in a cold place until ready for use. Always shake the dressing thoroughly before pouring over a salad.

# 12
# MIXING IT UP

## From Arm Fatigue to Leisure Time

Many a kitchen drawer has been known to overflow in its attempt to house too many kitchen gadgets. Usually designed for a single purpose, these gizmos promise efficiency—a solution to save wasted time while cooking. While home cooks today may find themselves accumulating more contraptions than they can store, kitchen gadgets are not a new phenomenon. From the can opener to the food chopper, many kitchen tools we utilize today were developed and patented in the nineteenth century.[1]

**The Barnett Company in Kenosha sold Dover eggbeaters for eight cents apiece in 1915.**
*Telegraph-Courier*, September 2, 1915

Anyone who has beaten egg whites to stiff peaks manually using a simple wire whisk understands why the invention of the mixer, and even its nonelectric predecessors, revolutionized the kitchen. After centuries of tired arms, Ralph Collier paved the way to easier egg beating in the United States with the apparatus he patented in 1856.[2] His eggbeater was a stationary table-top machine manually powered with a hand crank. Three years later, a handheld, rotary whisking device was patented.[3] Initially developed by James F. and Edward P. Monroe, this gadget was marketed by the Dover Stamping Company after it purchased the patent. The product is still known as a Dover eggbeater and was available in 1915 for just eight cents.[4]

The turn of the twentieth century was an inventive era, and people were interested in new and improved technologies they could bring into their kitchens. In 1900, the *Eagle River Review* reported on a new portable eggbeater.[5] Invented in New Zealand, this new hope for weary wrists was a sealable tube with spiraled metal blades on the inside. In practice, the cook would add the eggs, seal the tube, and then shake it while managing other kitchen tasks. It could also be set aside and picked up again without making a mess. Less portable but arguably faster was the pull-cord eggbeater drum

This portable eggbeater was featured as a new kitchen utensil in the *Eagle River Review* in 1900. *Eagle River Review*, September 20, 1900

highlighted in the *Wauwatosa News*.[6] This gadget promised a simple and novel way to beat an egg: "By merely pulling a flexible cord attached to the drum of the implement the blades are made to revolve both ways with great rapidity."[7]

Just when it seemed impossible to come up with yet another way of beating eggs, electricity transformed kitchens across the country. In a 1908 column discussing "Interesting New Inventions," the *Grant County Herald* spoke of a revolutionary addition to commercial kitchens that would soon be introduced to private households. Electricity, the fad that was being "used for almost every purpose under the sun," was now being used to beat eggs: "By pressing the button the beater revolves swiftly in the bowl, and as the power and the speed of the stroke does not vary the eggs are beaten with unusual consistency."[8] Not only could the task be managed without significant effort, it could also be done better—all with the simple push of a button.

# Mayonnaise

*Watertown Republican*, February, 25, 1874[9]

Makes approximately 1 cup

3 egg yolks

¼ teaspoon salt

¼ teaspoon white pepper

1 cup neutral flavor oil (grapeseed or canola work well), plus more if needed

2 tablespoons white wine vinegar

Beat the egg yolks in a bowl. Add salt and pepper.

MAYONNAISE DRESSING.—A nice dressing for chicken or lobster salad is made thus : Break the yolks of three raw eggs into a salad bowl, add a little salt and white pepper; stir it with a wooden spoon with the right hand, while with the left you add, very slowly, about half a pint of pure salad-oil poured from the bottle held in the left hand. Beat it for twenty minutes and add pepper and salt to your taste. Beat the whites of two eggs to a stiff froth and stir rapidly into the dressing. Now add about two large spoonfuls of vinegar, more or less, according to its strength, and blend all thoroughly together until it is as smooth as glass ; if not so, add a few drops of cold water to mingle the whole mixture.

While continuously stirring, slowly pour in the oil to incorporate it. Beat until you reach the desired mayonnaise texture. Add more oil, if needed. Pour in vinegar and stir until the mixture is smooth.

Note: Disregard additional instructions given in the original recipe and do not add beaten egg white. The fragrance and fluffy texture are rather off-putting.

# BAKED THINGS
## AND SANDWICHES

# 13

# HOT AND QUICK OR COOL AND SLOW

## Demystifying Historical Cooking Temperatures

According to one 1867 recipe, the perfect oven temperature for baking cornbread is a hot oven.[1] To a contemporary home baker, historical temperature descriptions can be cryptic, particularly if they come from a time when oven thermometers were not yet used. Most nineteenth-century people cooked and baked on and in wood-burning kitchen stoves. This required a baker to understand not only how to use a specific oven model and how to make and keep a fire of the correct size, but also the temperatures needed for any given recipe. Many baking instructions did not include any information concerning temperature whatsoever. Some newspaper articles offered tips to help home bakers make decisions about oven temperatures based on ingredients: "The correct temperature of the oven for various cake mixtures is often a vexed question for the amateur cook. A cake which is made with butter needs a moderate oven; a cake made without butter . . . a quick oven. For small cakes and cookies the oven should be moderately quick. . . . If the cake browns quickly after going into the oven, there is too much heat. Remove a lid from the top of the stove or put into the oven a dish containing cold water."[2]

One problem, however, was how a home baker would know when an oven had reached the intended temperature. The quantity of newspaper articles dealing with exactly this question throughout the late nineteenth century and well into the twentieth suggests that determining oven temperatures was an ongoing struggle. In 1884, the

*Wood County Reporter* taught its readers about a "baker's old-fashioned method of testing the temperature of an oven": "He throws flour on the floor. If it blackens without taking fire the heat is considered sufficient. It might be supposed that this is too high a temperature, as the object is to cook the flour, not to burn it. But we must remember that the flour which has been prepared for baking is mixed with water, and the evaporation of this water will materially lower the temperature of the dough itself."[3] This method was still popular in 1916 when the *Wausau Pilot* printed an article on "How to Test an Oven before You Burn Your Cake."[4]

According to a 1903 story printed in the *Eagle River Review,* some expert bakers were able to tell the temperature of their ovens "by simply touching the handle of the oven door."[5] Amateurs with less experience judging the temperature of hot iron by touch were advised to insert a piece of white paper or some cornmeal (as an alternative

**This scene accompanied a 1924 USDA article on how the size and construction of an oven makes a difference in baking.** *Eagle River Review,* October 23, 1924

to the aforementioned flour) into the oven instead. The time these items took to brown indicated the temperature.

By the 1920s, modernization was on the rise. In 1922, the US Department of Agriculture (USDA) published baking tips and conversion lists intended to aid home cooks transitioning to the standardized scale of Fahrenheit for temperatures in the kitchen.[6] A moderate oven was now 350 to 375 degrees Fahrenheit, and a hot oven was determined to mean "400°F, or a little more."[7] Most households made this transition gradually. By 1925, articles were still being printed making a case for the importance of thermometers in the kitchen to ensure quality and consistent results. While many recipes had since been converted to include cooking temperatures in Fahrenheit, many home bakers continued to rely on their tried-and-true methods. An article prepared by the USDA in 1925 described the advantages of exact temperatures for the "modern housekeeper": "Cookbooks intended to meet requirements no longer tell her to 'bake in a moderate oven,' leaving her to guess just what 'moderate' may mean.... Indispensable, therefore to accurate cookery is a dependable thermometer."[8]

Lucky for today's bakers, contemporary ovens boast not just thermometers but also thermostats, which enable the oven to maintain an even temperature and allow us to step away without worrying about opening stove lids, adding water to the stove, or putting more wood on the fire. The creative descriptions of oven temperatures in historical recipes give us a new appreciation for modern technology and offer a glimpse into how much work and frustration could be involved in baking, say, a simple loaf of bread. Not only did home bakers have to be vigilant around their stoves, they probably also had to settle for and eat many failed baked goods.

| Oven Temperature Equivalencies[9] | |
|---|---|
| DESCRIPTION | °F |
| Cool | 200 |
| Very Slow | 250 |
| Slow | 300 to 325 |
| Moderately Slow | 325 to 350 |
| Moderate | 350 to 375 |
| Moderately Hot | 375 to 400 |
| Quick/Hot | 400 to 450 |
| Very Hot | 450 to 500 |

# Crackers

*Dodgeville Chronicle*, May 16, 1873[10]
Makes 20 to 30 crackers

1 cup cold butter, cut into small cubes

8 cups flour

2 teaspoons salt

2–3 cups ice water

—Recipe for Crackers.—Butter, one cup; salt, one teaspoon; flour, two quarts. Rub thoroughly together with the hand, and wet up with cold water; beat well, and beat in flour to make quite brittle and hard; then pinch off pieces and roll out each cracker by itself, if you wish them to resemble bakers' crackers.

Preheat oven to 400°F. Rub butter, flour, and salt thoroughly together by hand. You can also use a food processor to save time. Slowly add ice water, a little bit at a time, until the dough becomes quite brittle and hard. Either pinch off pieces and roll them out individually, or roll out all of the dough until it is about ⅜-inch thick. Crackers may be cut using cookie cutters or a knife, depending on the desired shape.

Place crackers on a baking sheet and bake for 15 to 17 minutes. Remove from oven before they begin to brown. Let them cool before serving.

# (14)
# THE MANY FACES
# OF SOURDOUGH

## A Different Perspective on the History of a Bread

Naturally leavened bread made with a fermented sourdough starter has been around for millennia, which is probably why most historic newspapers did not bother printing recipes for such a well-known staple. Most readers would have already had that knowledge, and they probably would have been somewhat experienced bakers, as well. However, historic newspapers reveal that people used the term *sourdough* in different contexts—and not always in reference to baked goods.

During the Klondike Gold Rush that took place between 1896 and 1899, many miners carried pouches containing sourdough starter, which allowed them to bake loaves of fresh bread. The temperature of their bodies kept the starter alive in the harsh climate of Alaska and the Yukon. This earned the men the nickname "sourdoughs," which stuck for quite some time. Jack London's *Burning Daylight*, which appeared as a serialized novel in local newspapers and was published in book form in 1910, is one of many narratives that perpetuated not only the history of the Gold Rush but also the moniker: "Other sourdoughs, who had struck it rich in excess of all their dreams, shook their heads gloomily, warned him that he would go broke, and declined to invest in so extravagant a venture."[1] Sourdoughs were immortalized in fiction, and the term was commonly used in news stories for decades. In 1919, the *Eagle River Review* reported on a home for the elderly in Sitka where many aging sourdoughs now lived.[2]

In German-language newspapers, the term *Sauerteig* was not used to describe a person but was often used as a metaphor. A 1908 article covering socialism in Germany referred to discontent among the people as the sourdough allowing the socialist loaf to rise.[3] In 1911, Milwaukee's *Der Sonntagsbote* printed a speech delivered by the bishop of Toledo, Ohio, Joseph Schrembs, who urged his fellow Catholics to be the sourdough of Jesus Christ's doctrine of salvation.[4] Once in a while, a historic newspaper mentions someone with the surname Sauerteig, and if you are lucky, you can find a rare story on the origin of the sourdough with an added recipe, allowing us to continue the long tradition of breadmaking.[5]

# Pumpernickel

*Nord Stern,* December 22, 1916[6]

Makes 1 loaf

- 1 pound coarse rye flour, divided (Note: If you are able to, purchase rye berries and use a mill to make your own. The berries should be barely crushed. Pieces of the grain should be visible in the finished product. A 2:1 ratio of coarse ground rye flour to regular ground rye flour yields a traditional loaf of pumpernickel.)
- ⅓ ounce sourdough starter
- 2 teaspoons salt

Man bereite den Pumpernickel aus zweimal aeschrotenem nicht gesiebtem Roggen, also sammt der Kleie, mache den Teig am Abend vorher an. Man nimmt zwei Drittel des zum Backen bestimmten Mehles und vermengt es mit Sauerteig (auf 10 Pfund Mehl rechnet man 3 Unzen Sauerteig und ungefähr 2½ bis 3 Quarts Wasser, welches im Sommer 79—81 Grad Fahrenheit, im Winter 86 Grad Wärme haben muß). Am nächsten Morgen knete man das letzte Drittel Mehl mit hinein, läßt den Teig noch zwei Stunden an warmem Orte stehen und sticht ihn dann zu Broten aus. 2. Man thue 1½ Pfund grobes Roggenmehl in eine tiefe Backschüssel, füge eine Handvoll Salz und den sechsten Theil einer Tafel Hefe

Mix ⅔ pound of flour with starter and 1 quart water. Let rise in a warm spot overnight (8 to 12 hours).

In the morning, knead in remaining ⅓ pound flour and salt. Cover and let dough rise for another 2 hours in a warm place. Form loaf and bake at 350°F until a hard crust forms, about 1 hour and 45 minutes.

# 15

# BETWEEN TWO SLICES OF BREAD

## The Evolution of Sandwiches

For many, sandwiches bring to mind quintessential American cuisine. Although they don't begin to be mentioned in US cookbooks until the early nineteenth century, they have been around for much longer, with some attributing the invention to the fourth Earl of Sandwich in the mid-1700s.[1] If you define a sandwich as bread with a topping, though, they have been eaten for thousands of years by people of different cultures before that name was attached to them.

In Wisconsin, simple sandwiches began to appear in newspapers around the late 1860s when they were gaining in popularity after the Civil War. Sandwich recipes that made use of a variety of ingredients—were mentioned more and more frequently in Wisconsin newspapers

SANDWICHES.—A contemporary thus explains the origin of sandwiches: Lord Sandwich, when Minister of State, having passed twenty-four hours at a public gaming table, was so obsorbed in play during the whole time, that he ate nothing but a bit of beef between two slices of toasted bread. This delicacy was, and is to this day, called by the name of the minister who invented it.

*Grant County Herald*, August 6, 1867

into the 1880s. While sandwich recipes from the 1860s often called for ham, beef, or cheese on bread, recipes that appeared in the press twenty years later include fillings such as sardines, grouse, tomatoes, and raw beef.

As the end of the nineteenth century approached, the popularity of sandwiches continued to increase in the United States. Newspapers in Wisconsin responded to the growing interest by featuring recipes and articles such as "How to Make Good

Sandwiches," which appeared in the *Mineral Point Tribune* in 1892.[2] Many of the recipes contained new and exciting ideas, such as salmon sandwiches or different varieties of chocolate sandwiches. Enthusiasm for—and innovation related to—the bread-encased meal seemed to be endless as its reputation evolved from cheap travel food to a trendy and experimental delicacy. One 1893 article noted that "the crusty slices of greasy bread, with a muscular slice of beef or rare ham between, have been retired from good society."[3] More extravagant sandwiches earned a new, fashionable place in the culinary world through the late 1890s and into the 1900s.

The Progressive Era, beginning around 1900, ushered in a new age that included heightened interest in outdoor activities and a more casual lifestyle, as opposed to the rigidity of the Victorian era that began in 1837. The sandwich became the perfect food item for a picnic outing or a luncheon hosted by a "Gibson Girl"—a vision of the ideal American woman popular at the time—for her friends. The *Vernon County Censor* captured the attitude of early twentieth-century Americans and their sand-wiches, stating "Sandwiches are essentially summerfare. They are eaten in the woods, by the seashore, on the hillside, and mountain tops."[4]

With the invention of presliced bread in 1928, sandwiches truly became cemented into the American diet.[5] The convenience of a presliced loaf made sandwiches the easiest meal to throw together for lunches, send to school with children, and pack for trips and outings. According to a US food survey published in 2015, nearly half of all American adults enjoy a sandwich on an average day.[6] Resurrecting historical recipes for this beloved meal may be just the thing to keep it that way.

# Ham Sandwiches

*Manitowoc Pilot,* September 5, 1912[7]

Makes 8 to 10 sandwiches

1 ½ pounds cold boiled ham, finely
   chopped

3 sour pickles, finely chopped

1 tablespoon mustard

2 tablespoons butter, softened, plus
   extra for buttering bread

Dash black pepper

1 loaf bread (see Pumpernickel recipe
   on page 66)

Ham Sandwiches.—Put a pound and a half of ham, cold boiled, and a small sour pickle through a food chopper, add a tablespoonful of made mustard, a dash of pepper and two tablespoonfuls of butter. Mix thoroughly and spread on buttered bread.

*Nellie Maxwell.*

Mix ham and pickles in a bowl. Add mustard, butter, and pepper. Mix thoroughly and spread on buttered bread.

# 16

# KEEPING THINGS FRESH

## Bread in a Historical Kitchen

There are few things more frustrating than finding a loaf of bread has gone stale before you've had the chance to use all of it. Modern preservatives can give us a good week before our bread starts to become less than fresh, but before the introduction of such ingredients, bread had to be consumed much faster.

**An ad for Cream City flour and bread boxes published in 1913.** *Wauwatosa News*, March 21, 1913

Wisconsin's newspapers provided plenty of tips for readers on how to extend the freshness of their bread. Many advised readers to store their bread with half of an apple. As the *Wauwatosa News* explained in 1922, the moisture in the fruit was intended to keep the bread from drying out: "A cut apple placed in the bread box will give forth just enough moisture to keep the bread and cake fresh."[1] The trick of storing bread with a potato, suggested by the *Vernon County Censor* in 1916, was based on the same assumption that moisture would help keep the bread: "Wash a potato, wipe dry and put it in your bread pan. It will keep the bread fresh for days."[2]

An important factor in maintaining bread's freshness was the place it was stored. The bread box, a common feature of historical kitchens, was praised as the ideal place to keep a loaf. Bread boxes create a controlled environment that can prevent bread from prematurely drying out or getting moldy.

Allegedly, even if your bread box had been left open and your bread had not been stored with an apple or potato, all was not lost. Readers whose bread had gone stale were recommended to soak it in milk and re-bake it: "A dry loaf of bread, milk-soaked, can be re-baked and will be found as good as new."[3] In our opinion, turning hardened bread into breadcrumbs for a nice roast (see "Sharing Local Recipes" on page 116) might be a better option than attempting to re-bake it. Investing in a bread box, however, may still be useful for contemporary bread lovers.

# Pimento Sandwiches

*Wausau Pilot*, June 15, 1922[4]

Makes 12 sandwiches

1 pound American cheese, grated

1 (4-ounce) can pimento peppers, drained

2 hard-boiled eggs

About 1 cup mayonnaise (see Mayonnaise
    recipe on page 57)

¼ cup butter, softened, for buttering bread

1 loaf bread

1 head lettuce

> SANDWICH FILLING—One pound of American cheese, one small can of pimento, two hard boiled eggs chopped very fine. To this add enough salad dressing to make the filling creamy. Spread on lettuce leaf between thin slices of buttered bread. These sandwiches made a very good foundation for Sunday night supper during the warm weather.

Blend cheese, peppers, and eggs in a food processor until mixed. Add mayonnaise (enough to make the filling creamy) and blend again.

Spread the mixture on a slice of buttered bread. Add lettuce and an additional slice of bread for a closed sandwich.

# THE COMMERCIALIZATION OF CHEESE

## From Homestead Cultures to Factory Products

Wisconsin has a storied cheesemaking history. As early as 1842, the *Southport Telegraph* recorded that "in none of the Eastern states, do cows give as much milk (if regularly milked) or of as rich a quality, as do those running on the prairies of Northern Illinois, and Southern Wisconsin; and that in no country can extensive dairy operations be conducted with equal profit."[1] During this time, Europeans who immigrated to what would become the Dairy State brought with them generations-old cheesemaking recipes, and Wisconsin's newspapers published instructions to help farming families make the most of their dairy product. Though cheesemaking came to be widespread throughout the state, it was initially done on a small scale and for personal use, mainly to preserve a homestead's dairy yield, as milk, cream, and butter all spoiled more quickly than cheese.

Prior to the Civil War, Wisconsin's primary agricultural industry was grain, but with crop failures, pest infestations, and growing competition from the grain industry out West, the state turned its focus to dairy in the 1860s. By 1899, Wisconsin was well established as a "dairy state" with over "90 percent of Wisconsin farms rais[ing] dairy cows."[2] With this shift came Wisconsin's first commercial cheese operations and the beginning of standardization in cheesemaking across the state. As the *Kenosha Telegraph* reported in 1864, making cheese in a factory allowed for "uniformly good quality, with very little variation in the flavor—a thing impossible where each dairyman makes his own cheese."[3] Factory-produced cheese also fetched a higher price than the non-commercial product. In 1866, the *Dodgeville Chronicle* attested that commercial cheese was able to get a whole "cent or more on the pound."[4] The individuals opening these larger facilities mainly came from New York State, where eight hundred cheese factories were located by 1869, and they brought with them extensive knowledge on the process.[5]

Under the guidance of experienced commercial cheesemakers, Wisconsin's dairy industry began to flourish. By 1915, the state produced more than half of the country's cheese, and by 1923, Wisconsin was producing about 271,746,274 pounds of the product, valued at $4,457,780 (more than $77 million today).[6] To this day, cheese remains an important tradition in the state, and one of Wisconsin's fine local cheeses would lend itself perfectly to the preparation of an authentic historical cheese and English walnut sandwich.

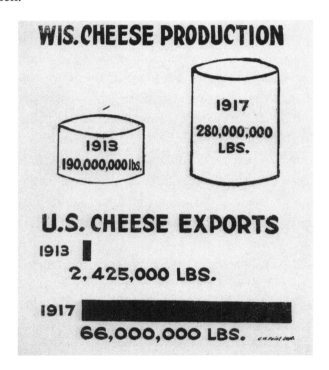

Illustrations showing the increase in Wisconsin's
cheese production and exports between 1913 and 1917.
*Iowa County Democrat*, November 21, 1918

# Cheese and English Walnut Sandwiches

*Wausau Pilot,* June 29, 1922[7]

Makes 6 to 8 sandwiches

¼ pound butter, softened

½ pound cheese, grated

Salt and black pepper, to taste

¼ pound English walnuts, finely
   chopped

1 loaf of bread

CHEESE AND ENGLISH WALNUT SANDWICHES--One-half pound grated cheese, one quarter pound of butter, one quarter pound English walnuts, salt and pepper. Cream the butter, add the seasoning and grated cheese gradually, then mix in the nuts which should be cut very fine; spread mixture on slices of bread and press together in pairs.

Cream butter by hand, then add cheese gradually. Add salt and pepper to taste. Stir nuts into mixture. Spread on slices of bread and press together in pairs.

# VEGETARIAN
# DISHES

# 18

## PLANNING AND PLANTING

### Setting Up a Home Garden

With today's steady availability of produce in supermarkets, gardening has largely become a hobby. But this was not always the case. Historically, people depended on their garden plots for regular access to fresh produce. Wisconsin newspapers encouraged home gardeners by printing advice tailored to this audience. Garden plans, such as one printed in a 1918 issue of the *Wood County Reporter*, were intended to help the average American family save money and labor, and they illustrated how a garden of any size could be used efficiently: "In this plan all the vegetables named are planted in rows across from the inside lateral rows of strawberries. As rapidly as each kind of pea matures and the crop is over, kale is planted in its place. The ground to be used for tomatoes is first planted with onion sets."[1]

The beginning of the twentieth century introduced many changes to the lives of average Americans. Advances in transportation and the industrialization of agriculture (see "Landreth's Legacy" on page 36) created an environment in which grocery stores could flourish by providing affordable kitchen staples that were reliably in stock, often regardless of the season. As many Americans began to rely more heavily on these commercial methods of obtaining their food, World War I began, and home gardens experienced a resurgence as the government urged citizens to conserve resources and maintain the home front by growing a portion of their own food. Articles with titles such as "Don't Neglect the Garden; Country Will Be Benefited If Each Lot Is Made a Permanent Food Producer" urged Americans to take up a plot on their own land.[2]

These home gardens, often called kitchen gardens, provided food for the everyday needs of a household. Harkening back to the gardens of early homesteads in the area, wartime plots were often near the home, as that location was most convenient for the garden caretaker, who was usually responsible for the domestic tasks of the household as well: "The work of caring for the garden is usually done at spare times, and for this reason alone the location should be near the dwelling."[3]

Coincidentally, this resurgence in home gardens was happening at the same time that domestic labor had begun to be studied and taught in a scientific context as home economics. As advancing modernity affected domestic life, it also spilled over into the gardening recommendations and plans of the early twentieth century. In an effort to make gardens more efficient, garden plans often called for vegetables that would prioritize nutrition and return on investment. The summer squash, for example, was advertised as a good plant for the home garden: "Two distinct types of squashes are commonly grown in home gardens—the summer squash, the fruits of which are used while they are young and tender, and the fall and winter squashes, which are ripened and used during the winter months. The small-growing summer squashes are best adapted to planting in the average garden."[4]

Today, urban and rural home gardeners may have access to new plant varieties that have been adapted to thrive in the local climate, have an improved flavor, or yield a better harvest. However, tips provided in historic newspapers can still help when it comes to fighting a squash bug infestation or planning the layout for the next season's garden.

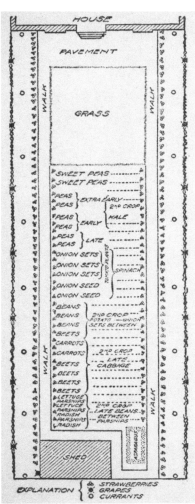

**A detailed plan for a home garden published in a 1918 USDA article.**
*Wood County Reporter,* April 25, 1918

EXTRA! EXTRA! EAT ALL ABOUT IT!

# Summer Squash

*Wauwatosa News*, January 10, 1908[5]

Makes 2 servings

4 medium summer squash

3 teaspoons salt

1 tablespoon olive oil

⅓ cup shredded Swiss cheese

⅓ cup tomato sauce

**New Recipe for Cooking Squash.**

Summer Squash, Columbine—Cut into quarters a large, solid summer squash; take out the seeds and pare. Slice lengthwise into pieces half an inch thick and sprinkle each piece thickly with salt. Let stand an hour to take out the water. At the end of that time fold the slices in a towel and wipe dry. Fry to a light brown in about an inch of hot cooking oil. When all the slices are fried, place them in a baking dish in layers well-sprinkled with grated Swiss cheese. Cover all with tomato sauce and bake for fifteen minutes. Serve in the same dish. Egg-plant also is delicious used in this way.

Preheat oven to 375°F. Peel squash, quarter lengthwise, and remove seeds.

Slice lengthwise into half-inch-thick pieces. Sprinkle with salt and let stand for 1 hour. Pat dry and pan fry in oil until browned.

When all slices are fried, place them in a small baking dish one layer at a time, sprinkling Swiss cheese between layers.

Cover all with tomato sauce and bake for 15 minutes. Serve hot.

# 19

# A HISTORICAL STORAGE SOLUTION

## Root Cellars

What was once a standard place to store food in any rural household or farm is mostly unfamiliar today. In the days before electric refrigeration, root cellars were necessary to keep produce fresh and were as common as a barn on any countryside homestead. In fact, it would have been odd to find properties listed for sale without mention of a root cellar. For instance, among this DeSoto house's charms were "10 rooms; root cellar; wash room; double porch; upper story screened; two cisterns; pump in kitchen; village well at corner of lot; terraced garden."[1] And the hopeful sellers of this "40-acre farm 3 ½ miles from Ladysmith" boasted that it was "all tillable, 2 acres stumped and about 20 acres cut off, clay loom soil: ½ mile from school. House 16 x 24 worth about $400, log barn 18 x 24, poultry house, good root cellar; good well and iron pump. Price $800; only $350 down, balance 6 percent interest."[2]

The advent of electricity in households at the turn of the twentieth century eventually meant that refrigerators replaced root cellars. However, many home cooks trying recipes like the ones in this book continued to leave their houses and walk over to their root cellars to retrieve their ingredients well into the 1940s, when electric refrigerators became a common feature in American households.[3]

People created root cellars by digging into the earth at the edge of a hill or bluff, if one was available. These small rooms usually had dirt floors, and the humidity from the dirt helped preserve the food they contained. The walls and ceiling were usually constructed with stone, such as limestone or concrete, which helped regulate temperatures and keep out pests. When there was no elevated piece of land to dig into, some homeowners would dig straight into the ground as for a traditional basement, building a mound on top of the structure with the excavated dirt. In 1916, the *Northern Wisconsin Advertiser* outlined what should be considered when constructing a root cellar:

> In making the pit, the following main items should be arranged for:
>
> • Ventilation—There should be a free circulation of air at all times.
>
> • Heat—The temperature should never be allowed to fall below the freezing point. It is best to keep it just above freezing.
>
> • Walls and Floor—The walls are usually concrete. The floor should be left uncemented if possible, because the moisture from the dirt will keep vegetables from drying out.[4]

As the name suggests, root cellars were especially well equipped to store root vegetables. When the cellars were built with care, the temperature could be regulated to prevent overheating in the summer and freezing in the winter. In these conditions, vegetables—such as carrots, turnips, and potatoes, as called for in this recipe—could last nearly a year and sometimes kept families from starving in the winter. While many of us may think of the root cellar as an antiquated thing of the past, others are rediscovering this tried-and-true dugout and its ability to help foster a more sustainable and self-sufficient lifestyle.

# Creamed Potatoes with Cheese Sauce

*Iowa County Democrat,* November 21, 1918[5]

Makes 4 servings

1 cup plus 2 tablespoons milk, divided

1 ½ tablespoons flour or ⅕ tablespoon
    cornstarch

½ teaspoon salt

⅛ teaspoon white pepper

⅓ teaspoon baking soda

¼ cup cottage cheese

1 pimento or ½ bell pepper, chopped

3–4 sprigs parsley, chopped

3 medium russet potatoes, boiled

Creamed potatoes with cheese sauce —Potatoes boiled and sliced in the usual way, and served with a white sauce made of one cupful milk, one and one-half tablespoonfuls flour or one-half tablespoonful cornstarch, one-third teaspoonful salt, dash of white pepper, one-quarter cup cottage cheese, one-third teaspoonful soda. Mix the soda in a small amount of milk and add to cheese to neutralize. Prepare white sauce as usual and add cheese mixture when sauce is well cooked. A little chopped pimento or parsley may be added. Pour over potatoes, beat well, and serve immediately.

Make a white sauce by heating 1 cup milk in a pot and mixing in flour or cornstarch slowly to prevent lumps from forming. Add salt and pepper.

Combine baking soda with the remaining 2 tablespoons milk and add to cottage cheese. Stir the mixture into the white sauce. Add pimento or bell pepper and parsley to the sauce.

Slice potatoes and arrange in a casserole dish. Pour sauce over potatoes and serve immediately.

# 20

# HELPFUL HINTS AND CROP REPORTS

## Spreading Agricultural Information

When looking through an old newspaper, you might be surprised by the amount of agricultural information contained within the pages. While not commonly associated with newspapers today, agriculturally focused information—along with news articles, social columns, and recipes—was a common feature in Wisconsin newspapers. Farmers on both a large and small scale could find tips, advice, planting schedules, and more at their fingertips.

## Helpful Hints for Our Modern Farmers

A regular department of THE REVIEW that will provide much valuable information to the dairymen, stock raisers and agriculturists of Vilas County and vicinity

*Eagle River Review*, June 7, 1923

Beginning in the 1920s, the *Eagle River Review* ran a section called Helpful Hints for Our Modern Farmers, which the paper described as "a regular department of *The Review* that will provide much valuable information to the dairymen, stock raisers, and agriculturalists of Vilas County and vicinity."[1] Articles in sections like these covered a myriad of topics, from diseased black raspberry bushes to how to "control melon aphid with nicotine sulfate" to various livestock feeding methods. Helpful Hints also aided readers in the growing of crops like spinach, providing advice on when to sow the leafy vegetable, what type of fertilizer to use, and how to prevent pests. The newspapers that carried agriculturally focused columns and articles were most often published in the areas of Wisconsin with the most agricultural activity, and included the *River Falls Journal, Eagle River Review, Vernon County Censor,* and *Grant County Herald,* to name a few.

Until the 1930s, when the radio became commonplace in US households, newspapers were the only available medium for spreading information in a timely manner.[2] For many farmers, reading the paper was the best way to stay current on the latest findings in their line of work. The US Department of Agriculture (USDA) was well aware of this fact, and it printed its research findings, recommendations, and warnings in local newspapers to guarantee the information would be considered by farmers who grew the crops that fed the nation.

Press representatives grab copies of a newly released crop report in this image from a 1918 USDA article. *Washburn Times,* July 25, 1918

The monthly crop report release day at the USDA was filled with excitement. Journalists crowded the room to get their hands on paper copies to study. Then, the reporters would convey the information to their constituents:

> On "crop reporting day" at an hour set months in advance, newspaper and press association representatives gather in the main building of the department of agriculture. . . . Shortly before the moment[,] set copies of the completed crop reports are placed on a table, face down, and each newspaper man gets his hand on one. At the signal, given by a high official of the Department, the newspaper men get to their telephones and in a very few minutes more the coveted information is being read in every large market in the United States and the next day, at the latest, it is available in every community of the United States and in the larger markets of foreign countries.[3]

The reports contained information on the "production, condition, shipment, prices, demand, and quality" of various crops, which affected not only farmers and consumers but the global market, as the *Washburn Times* stated in 1918: "Dependence of a large part of the world upon American farm production has focused public attention upon the crop reports of the United States Department of Agriculture."[4]

To this day, the USDA continues to publish crop reports, which are available to anyone with access to the internet—a stark difference from the way similar information used to be conveyed. Still, it wasn't long ago that newspapers, even small ones, were vital organs of geopolitical communication and thereby played an important part in feeding the nation.

# Spinach Balls
*Our Land–La Nostra Terra*, August 30, 1913[5]
Makes 4 servings

## Spinach Balls

1 cup cooked spinach, chopped

2 tablespoons butter

2 tablespoons flour

1 tablespoon cream

1/4 teaspoon salt

1/4 teaspoon black pepper

1/4 teaspoon mace

Pinch sugar

2 eggs, well beaten

Spinach Balls.—Press liquid from a cupful of cooked and chopped spinach. Reheat it with two tablespoonfuls each of butter and flour and a tablespoonful of cream. Season with salt, pepper, sugar and mace. Take from the fire and add two well beaten eggs. Cool and form into balls. Let it simmer in boiling water five or six minutes, drain and add hot cream sauce in which are a few capers.

## Cream Sauce

1 tablespoon butter

1 tablespoon flour

1 cup cream

1 heaping teaspoon capers

Salt and black pepper, to taste

For spinach balls: Press liquid from spinach. Reheat spinach on medium low heat with butter, flour, and cream. Season with salt, pepper, mace, and sugar.

Remove from heat. Add eggs carefully, to prevent curdling. Let cool and form into balls, 1 3/4-inch in diameter.

In a pot, bring water to a simmer and cook spinach balls until they float, for 5 to 6 minutes, then remove from water.

For cream sauce: Melt butter in a small pot. Add flour and stir into a paste. Pour in cream and stir until smooth. Add capers, salt, and pepper. Pour sauce over hot spinach balls.

# 21

## MEATLESS MINCEMEAT AND POULTRY EXCEPTIONS

### The Rise of Modern Vegetarianism

Vegetarianism is not a modern concept. In both Eastern and Western cultures, people have been making the purposeful choice to abstain from consuming meat since as early as 600 BCE.[1] Wisconsin is not missing from the history of vegetarianism; some of the state's most famous inhabitants have been vegetarians, including Governor Robert M. La Follette, who adopted the diet during his time at the University of Wisconsin. As the *Baraboo News* quipped in 1906, "The discovery that La Follette is a vegetarian, may come as a relief to certain senators that had a fear that he might eat them alive."[2]

In Wisconsin newspapers, vegetarian eating habits were often met with criticism, if not outright suspicion. Articles aligned vegetarians with extreme ideologies, religious movements, and progressive beliefs, and some drew a connection between vegetarians and people who abstained from alcohol and tobacco. In 1885, the *Wood County Reporter* reported on the "Bible Church, of Sanford, England, [which] makes vegetarianism as well as teetotalism and total abstinence from tobacco an essential condition of its church and membership."[3] Local newspapers framed vegetarianism as a curiosity, providing Wisconsinites with descriptions of vegetarian restaurants in large cosmopolitan cities such as New York and London and marveling at those who dined in such establishments that "excluded all forms of animal food."[4]

The strangeness of vegetarianism eventually lost its novelty, and as the nineteenth century came to a close, public attention turned toward the diet as a possible form of healthy eating. Though the nutritional claims made at the time were sometimes dubious (see "All in the Name of Health" on page 30), articles argued both the health advantages and disadvantages of a vegetarian diet: "It is now agreed that meat eating is particularly the cause of many complaints; there is more or less poisonous matter remaining in the carcasses of animals caused by various chemical changes, and these toxic elements gradually affect those who make meat a staple article of diet."[5] This view was contrasted by claims that "vegetarianism tends to produce an excess of the albuminous element of the blood, . . . imparting a paleness and flabbiness to the tissues, a general delicacy of look, and want of stamina and power."[6]

## MEATLESS DIET HEALTHFUL

### Carnivorous Habits Said to Be Unnatural and Harmful to Human Beings.

It would be quite foolish to become discouraged on account of strikes which cause a rise in the price of meat. If the cost of flesh food went wholly beyond the means of man, there would be no good cause for despair. Meat is not a necessity of life. Many think it is both a luxury and an evil. At best it is a "matter of habit," like coffee, alcohol, tobacco, chewing gum or pie.

*River Falls Journal*, August 25, 1904

The concept of avoiding meat continued to gain momentum into the twentieth century. The meatpacking scandals that unfolded following the "embalmed" cans of beef sent to soldiers in the Spanish-American War sent the American public into a frenzy of meat-industry distrust. In Wisconsin, the *Eagle River Review* reported that in the conflict with Spain, more soldiers had died from the rancid beef than in battle.[7] Upton Sinclair's *The Jungle* was published shortly thereafter, and the ruthless exposé of the unsanitary and unsafe conditions in the US meatpacking industry led to the Meat Inspection Act of 1906.[8] Following the uproar, the public was less concerned with the health advantages of increasing the vegetable intake in their diets and more interested in meatless recipes as a way to avoid eating potentially harmful meat: "Vegetarians are making the most of the meat scandal. They are giving elaborate dinners and luncheons in the hope of adding converts to their lists."[9]

With this growing interest in plant-based eating, vegetarian and meatless recipes began to appear in newspapers with more frequency. The definition of vegetarianism was often nebulous, as a 1911 recipe for "Meatless Mince Meat" shows—though it technically did not contain meat, it did make use of suet, hardened animal fat.[10] Similarly, the "Meatless Monday" campaign of World War I (see "Cottage Cheese Propaganda" on page 178) encouraged civilians to refrain from eating meat to help feed the troops, but it did not always count poultry as meat.[11] Nevertheless, the growing public awareness around vegetarianism and decreasing rates of meat consumption led to many recipes for meat alternatives and delicious vegetable and legume creations, such as "Parsnip Croquettes" and a "Meatless Bean Soup."[12] Many readers may delight in the fact that historic newspapers contain a wealth of recipes that cater to even the strictest of vegetarian eaters and that historical cooking is not just for the meat and potato folk.

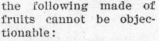
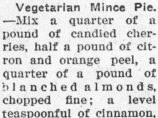

For the vegetarian, mince pies made in the ordinary way are not liked, but the following made of fruits cannot be objectionable:

Vegetarian Mince Pie. —Mix a quarter of a pound of candied cherries, half a pound of citron and orange peel, a quarter of a pound of blanched almonds, chopped fine; a level teaspoonful of cinnamon, four tablespoonfuls of sugar, the grated —rind of a lemon, the juice of two oranges, one cupful of crumbs, a teaspoonful of salt. Add sufficient orange or grape juice to moisten. Use the crumbs only as it is ready to use.

This recipe and others catering to a vegetarian diet appeared in Nellie Maxwell's Kitchen Cabinet column in 1917. *Eagle River Review*, November 30, 1917

# Baked Cowpeas and Cheese

*Northern Wisconsin Advertiser*, February 11, 1921[13]

Makes 4 servings

2 cups cooked cowpeas (black-eyed peas)

1 cup grated cheese (cheddar works well)

1 tablespoon finely chopped onion

1 tablespoon finely chopped green bell pepper

1–2 tablespoons butter, melted, divided

Preheat oven to 350°F. Press peas through a sieve to remove skins or use a food processor to blend the peas. Mix peas with cheese.

**Baked Cowpeas and Cheese.**

1 tablespoonful butter. 1 tablespoonful finely chopped sweet green pepper. 2 cupfuls cooked cowpeas.

1 tablespoonful finely chopped onion. 1 cupful grated cheese.

Press the peas through a sieve to remove the skins, and mix with the cheese. Cook the onion and pepper in the butter, being careful not to brown, and add them to the peas and cheese. Form the mixture into a roll, place on a buttered earthenware dish and cook in a moderate oven until brown, basting occasionally with butter and water. Serve hot or cold as a substitute for meat.

Cook onion and pepper in 1 tablesoon butter, being careful not to brown them, and add to the peas and cheese. Form the mixture into a roll, place in a small buttered casserole dish, and bake until brown, approximately 40 minutes. Baste occasionally with water and additional butter.

Serve hot or cold as a substitute for meat.

# MEAT DISHES

# 22
# PAPER BAG COOKING

## A Fad Long Forgotten

"Paper bag cookery and fireless cookers should be locked in a room together. They are both delusions," stated a *Washburn Times* article in 1912.[1] The *Times*'s jab at the popular cooking method came a year after Nicolas Soyer published his popular cookbook *Soyer's Paper-Bag Cookery*.[2] Inspired by the French way of preparing food *en papillotte*, meaning enveloped in paper, the British chef introduced a way for home chefs to cook everyday dishes in a paper bag.

According to this method, vegetables and meat would be completely enclosed in a paper bag, which allowed them to steam rather than bake in a hot oven. However, paper and heat don't always mix well, and Soyer included some tales of failed experiments in his book: "I put some meat, vegetables, and a little water into an envelope, and laid it on the iron shelf in the oven. The inevitable happened. The paper burnt, and soon afterwards it exploded."[3]

In October 1911, the *Watertown Leader* introduced paper bag cookery to its readers as a delicious way to prepare vegetables.[4]

**This image appeared alongside a series of paper bag cooking recipes published in Wabeno's *Northern Wisconsin Advertiser*.**
*Northern Wisconsin Advertiser*, April 12, 1912

The method caught on quickly as a trendy new way to prevent meals from drying out and to save time doing dishes. According to professional chefs, cooking in a bag was thought to be more sanitary than cooking in dishes or pans. The bag method also required less attention and fewer spices, kept flavors from mingling, and was all in all "a distinct gain for humanity."[5] From smothered chicken to stuffed onions, new and exciting paper bag recipes continued to arrive in Wisconsin households via newspapers throughout the early 1910s. In 1912, the Wabeno *Northern Wisconsin Advertiser* ran a series that devoted half a page each week to recipes that used the new way of cooking. And for those "interested ladies of Watertown" who did not yet feel comfortable trying out the novel method, the local gas and electric company hosted a paper bag cooking demonstration on May 6, 1912.[6]

Clearly, Soyer's concept was having an influence on Wisconsin kitchens, but as with most trends and fads, mockery was imminent. As the *Washburn Times* quipped, "There is a good deal of talk now about 'paper-bag cooking,' but without having tried it we shouldn't think a paper bag would taste good, no matter how it may be cooked."[7] Jokes began appearing in Wisconsin newspapers nearly as soon as the trend took off, and it ultimately became a pop culture reference. A few lines in a 1913 issue of the *Wood County Reporter* poked fun at the concept:

### The Lazy Way.

Mrs. Crawford—Why don't you try the new paper bag cooking?

Mrs. Crabshaw—I would, dear, if I thought it was as easy as getting the meals in a paper bag at the delicatessen store.[8]

After the trend faded, the *Vernon County Censor* reminisced about the paper bag cooking craze that swept the nation: "We bought recipe books and no end of bags. We liked the fad for a while and then we forgot."[9]

# Stuffed Onions (Cooked in a Paper Bag)

*Manitowoc Pilot,* November 21, 1912[10]

Makes 6 servings

Note: To prevent any modern glues and dyes from altering the taste or safety of your meal, use baking parchment paper and uncoated metal paper clips to make a bag.

6 medium yellow onions

½ pound ground pork

½ pound ground beef

¼ cup chopped pecans

3 sprigs parsley, chopped

1 teaspoon paprika

1 teaspoon salt

½ teaspoon black pepper

2 tablespoons butter, cut into 6 pats

Stuffed Onions.—Parboil a sufficient number of medium-sized onions for the meal, put them into cold water, drain and, when cold, remove the centers. Fill the onions with a savory stuffing or chopped ham, or nuts or bits of sausage; anything that will make a stuffing of sufficient flavor. Place in a buttered bag with a little water and butter, and bake for three-quarters of an hour. Remove from the bag to a hot vegetable dish, sprinkle with salt and pepper and serve with the sauce from the bag poured around them.

Preheat oven to 420°F (or the maximum temperature allowed for your parchment). Peel onions and parboil them for 15 minutes. Let them cool in cold water and, using a knife or apple corer and your fingers, remove the centers (about two-thirds of the onion). Chop half of the removed onion centers and add them to a bowl with ground pork and beef, pecans, parsley, paprika, salt, and pepper. Mix well and stuff the onions with the mixture.

Place the stuffed onions on half of a large sheet of baking parchment, top them with a pat of butter each, and fold over the other half of the parchment to create a bag. Double-fold two edges and fasten them with paper clips. Add ¼ cup water to the pouch and fold and fasten the third edge to seal it.

Bake for 45 minutes. Make sure that the paper is not touching the heating elements of your oven and check on your paper frequently to avoid disaster. Carefully remove the bag from the oven, cut open, and enjoy the aroma.

Serve onions drizzled with the sauce left at the bottom of the bag.

# 23

# WIRED WITH EXCITEMENT

## Cooking with Electricity

On Halloween in 1878, Kenosha residents opened page three of the newspaper and got an unexpected glimpse of the future. A short article predicted what seemed unthinkable at the time: the advent of electricity in private households around the world. While electricity was already starting to light up the streets of Paris, this author's vision of the future involved the indoor use of electricity, writing, "It may develop more highly special utilities, as for cooking and lighting interiors."[1]

News of innovations and advances related to electricity was soon published in other parts of the state as well. By 1890, the *Watertown Republican* reported on progress in the field, detailing new applications for the energy source such as an electric soldering iron or a fireman's electric hand lamp.[2] Just three years later, the same paper claimed that "one of the greatest advantages of the electric light is the absolute ease with which it can be turned either on and off, and to have this convenience in the kitchen will reduce the culinary art to a luxury, for it will be possible to regulate the heat just as easily as to regulate light."[3] Soon after, the front page of the *Eagle River Review* featured illustrations of electric appliances and what was called a "Model Electrical Kitchen."[4]

However, despite potential consumers' enthusiasm and growing interest in electricity during the late nineteenth century, the new technology came with a high price tag in its early years. Most publications agreed, "the difficulty of cooking by electricity is that the current cannot be always easily and cheaply attained."[5] In the decades before the United States had an expansive and affordable electrical grid, the electric stove remained an unattainable fantasy for the average American.

# ELECTRIC FIRELESS COOK STOVES

We cordially invite all of the ladies of Grand Rapids and vicinity to attend the Demonstration held in our new Store Building on Thursday, Friday and Saturday, demonstrating the actual workings of the Electric Fireless Cook Stoves and showing how to cook the various kinds of foods at a less cost than gas or gasoline and in a more efficient manner.

## The "Fireless" Cooker with a "College" Education

# Johnson & Hill Company
### HARDWARE DEPARTMENT

In 1911, this early electric stove was sold at Johnson & Hill Company in Wisconsin Rapids. *Wood County Reporter*, May 25, 1911

Though electricity in home kitchens was still out of reach for many in the 1890s, there was still intense excitement about the idea at the time. Research into the practicality of this novel way of cooking continued, and demonstrations at community events were organized to garner more public interest. The *Superior Times* mentioned with amazement in its 1892 "Fair Notes" that a buckwheat pancake served at the event had been prepared with electricity. "The electrical display was beyond all explanation," the paper proclaimed.[6]

It was not until the early 1910s, however, that the first advertisements for electric stoves appeared in Wisconsin newspapers. The Johnson & Hill Company hardware department in Wisconsin Rapids placed an advertisement for its Electric Fireless Cook Stoves in the *Wood County Reporter* in 1911.[7] What is striking about the advertisement is how little this electric stove resembled the other stoves of the time period. The small appliance looked like a wooden chest in which food items could be placed to cook. Perhaps this futuristic style of electric stove did not become prevalent in local kitchens because of its design, which likely struck consumers as unusual and unfamiliar. By the end of the decade, electric stoves such as the GE type K-30 Electric Range looked and operated very similarly to the traditional cookstoves that came before it.[8] This more familiar design was an easier sell to consumers, and it proved to be timeless—even our contemporary stoves bear resemblance to the 1919 model. It took about forty years after the first signs of the electrical revolution for the future to actually arrive, but electric stoves have been helping Americans whip up delicious dishes, such as Rice and Ham with Eggs, ever since.

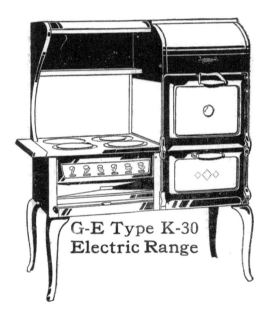

G-E Type K-30
Electric Range

This GE electric range could be purchased from the Janesville Electric Company in 1919.
*Wisconsin Tobacco Reporter*, May 30, 1919

# Rice and Ham with Eggs

*Wisconsin Weekly Blade*, September 7, 1916[9]

Makes 1 serving

1 cup cooked rice

¼ cup diced cooked ham

1 egg

Salt and black pepper, to taste

**Rice and Ham With Eggs.**

This dish may be served in individual dishes or not, as liked. Mince cold cooked ham, add to it either cold or hot plain boiled rice and when well mixed fill the individual dish or ramekin half full of the mixture; drop an egg on the top of each, season with salt and pepper to taste and bake in a quick oven until the egg is set. Serve hot in the dishes in which it was cooked.

Preheat oven to 400°F. Mix rice and ham in a medium bowl.

Fill oven-safe individual dish or ramekin with the rice mixture. Crack egg on the top.

Bake until the rice is hot and the egg has set, about 5 to 10 minutes. Season with salt and pepper. Serve hot.

# FOR THE LOVE OF PASTA

## A Historical Discourse on Texture

Food preferences can change over time. While children typically enjoy sweet things and find bitter foods distasteful, many grow to enjoy coffee as adults. But it is not just personal tastes that change with the passing years. Communal or societal changes in taste can be detected by comparing recipes throughout history. Modern recipes, for example, call for much more salt than those from the early nineteenth century. One interesting aspect of browsing old recipes is the difference in flavor combinations people seem to have enjoyed. Beyond flavor, preferences in texture also seem to have changed. While some people surely continue to enjoy anything jellied, most of us can probably agree that a mixture of gelatin, spinach, and onion juice would no longer appeal to the average salad lover.

**Time Table.**
Peas, tomatoes, rice, green corn, spinach and hard-boiled eggs require twenty minutes to boil.

Asparagus, cauliflower, squash, celery, macaroni, potatoes, young cabbage, twenty to thirty minutes to boil.

In 1900, the *Eagle River Review* advised readers to cook macaroni for twenty to thirty minutes. *Eagle River Review,* September 27, 1900

Another textural preference—which is not as easily detectable as a fondness for gelatin—becomes apparent after a close examination of the cooking times of a contemporary pantry staple: pasta. Many historical recipes called for it to be cooked until tender.

That is not unusual for today's standards, although many cooks now prefer to cook pasta al dente, allowing it to retain a certain degree of firmness. There is no mention of the phrase *al dente* in Wisconsin's historic newspapers, but there are some detailed recipes that grant us insight into what, exactly, was considered tender. An 1891 recipe for boiled macaroni, for example, reads: "Put macaroni into a porcelain-lined kettle; add a small onion chopped; boil in water about half an hour, stirring often."[1] From a contemporary standpoint, the recipe not only neglects adding salt to the pasta water but also calls for an excessive cooking time. When cooked for thirty minutes, dried pasta will become very soft and take on an eggier taste. The 1891 recipe was not the only cooking instruction calling for very-well-cooked pasta, either. Household tips printed in newspapers from 1898 and 1900 also suggested that ideal cooking times for macaroni were between twenty and thirty minutes.[2]

The fact that these recommendations were published when a growing number of Italian immigrants were settling in Wisconsin is peculiar. One might assume that Italian immigrants both introduced the dish to the state and made sure to pass along the proper cooking technique. Yet, although the growing Italian population—especially in Milwaukee—may have helped increase the availability of dried pasta in the state, advertisements for "Maccaroni" and "Vermicelli" at a Kenosha grocer's as early as 1850 suggest that Wisconsinites may have formed the habit of overcooking their pasta prior to the immigration wave.[3] Modern recipes reveal that a preference for al dente pasta now rules, but as tastes are bound to change over time, we can't know whether we will enter an era of mushiness again.

In 1850, the Kenosha Produce & Provision Store kept several types of pasta in stock.
*Kenosha Telegraph*, October 11, 1850

# Hamburg Spaghetti

*Watertown Weekly Leader*, February 16, 1915[4]

Makes 6 servings

## Meatballs

1 pound ground beef

1 egg

¼ cup dried bread crumbs

2 tablespoons grated onion

½ teaspoon salt

½ teaspoon paprika

Butter, for browning the meatballs

## Sauce

1 tablespoon butter

1 tablespoon flour

1 (28-ounce) can crushed tomatoes

1 onion, chopped

2 green bell peppers, chopped

2 sprigs parsley, chopped

## To Finish

12 ounces spaghetti

¾ cup shredded cheese (mozzarella works well)

Hamburg Spaghetti.—Take a pound of chopped steak, one egg, one-quarter cupful of bread crumbs, one teaspoonful of grated onion, salt and paprika to taste. Take a can of tomatoes for the sauce, add one onion sliced, one sweet green pepper chopped, two sprigs of parsley chopped, one pint of water, one teaspoonful of salt and paprika. Cook together the butter and flour, add to the tomatoes and seasoning and cook half an hour, put through a sieve into a casserole. Mix the meat with the seasonings and roll into balls. Brown them in a little hot butter and put them into the casserole. Cover and cook slowly for an hour. Cook spaghetti in salted water, drain and sprinkle with cheese and add to the casserole. Serve hot from the dish.

Preheat oven to 300°F.

For meatballs: Mix ground beef with egg, bread crumbs, and grated onion, and season with salt and paprika. Roll mixture into balls. In a pan, melt a little butter and brown the meatballs.

For sauce: In a sauce pan, combine butter and flour and cook until the roux starts to brown. Add add tomatoes, onion, bell peppers, and parsley. Cook for half an hour over medium heat.

Note: The original recipe calls for the sauce to be poured into a casserole dish through a sieve and to dispose of the vegetables. However, vegetable lovers who may enjoy keeping the vegetables can pour the sauce straight into the casserole dish.

Place meatballs on top of the sauce and cover the casserole dish. Bake for 1 hour.

Cook spaghetti in salted water, drain, and stir into the mixture in the casserole dish. Sprinkle with cheese and serve hot in the dish.

# (UN)PLEASING TO THE EYE

## Before the Age of Food Photography

The observant reader will likely have noticed a lack of historical photographs capturing the dishes re-created in this book. Visuals are essential for modern recipes, whether they are printed in a book, newspaper, or magazine or published online. Food photography is its own genre of the art form, evoking emotions and, ideally, physical reactions of the mouthwatering kind. Rest assured that you are not being denied these historical pictures—they simply never existed.

As printers began publishing the first newspapers in Wisconsin, photography was still in the early stages of its development. The film camera would not be invented for half a century, and daguerreotypes were the way to go for permanently fixed pictures. While they were popular for portraits, however, daguerreotypes were seldom used to snap pictures of food. Not only was the process of capturing an image much more elaborate at the time than it is now, but mass-printing such an image in newspapers would have been another time-consuming and laborious commitment.

News publications have almost always consisted of more than just words. Even early specimens featured artful mastheads, embellishments, decorative borders, and little images. These were printed using cuts, essentially metal or wooden stamps of illustrations, which could be embedded in the block of type making up a page. Newspapers could order generic cuts from printers' suppliers, such as the C. R. Gether Company in Milwaukee. Gether's 1907 catalog of electrotyped stock cuts spanned over 250 pages. Despite the abundant selection, cuts could function only as embellishment and could not capture specific dishes. Beautiful, detailed illustrations could be commissioned to be engraved by hand or etched into metal. Yet, while these pieces of art could be stunningly realistic, most publishers did not have the budget to pay for an engraver to intricately illustrate a dish to accompany an average recipe.

The process of photoengraving, which became more common in the second half of the nineteenth century, finally made it easier and cheaper to print photographs. Photoengraving is the process of transferring a fixed image onto a metal plate, often made of copper and coated in a light-sensitive substance. Through multiple acid washes, the image is etched into the metal, which can then be used as a printing plate. This process was soon refined to allow for half-tone printing, in which a photograph is reproduced as an arrangement of dots of different sizes, allowing the image to appear in grayscale rather than bitonal black and white.[1]

Despite these technological advances, local newspapers rarely made use of photoengraving, likely because it required a specific skillset. In 1896, an article in the *Wood County Reporter* was enthusiastic about the advantages photoengraving promised for the printing industry: "The present process of photoengraving carried out by good workmen, brings out excellent results."[2] However, good workmen probably were not available to many local publishers, and even if they were, photoengraving was still a lengthy process used mostly for special occasions. The Kenosha *Telegraph-Courier*, for example, featured twenty-three photographs printed using this technique in its

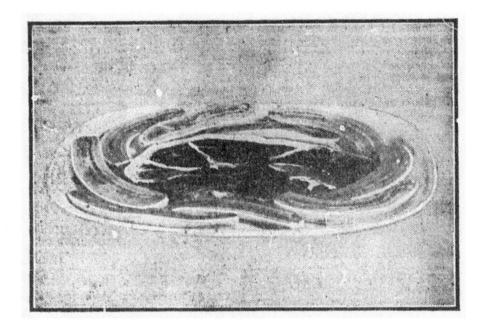

**This photograph of Barbecued Ham with Bananas appeared in a 1909 article
for young brides about housekeeping in Viroqua's *Vernon County Censor*.**
*Vernon County Censor*, August 25, 1909

semicentennial edition on May 29, 1890. A local photographer, Mr. Allderidge, had been commissioned to capture the city and then work with skilled photoengravers in Chicago to deliver the most visually impressive issue of the paper to date.[3]

Unfortunately, Mr. Allderidge failed to photograph any of the food people were eating in Kenosha around the turn of the century. And he was not the only photographer to refrain from doing so for a very long time. The fact that the following recipe came to readers with an accompanying photograph is, therefore, quite surprising and surely made Barbecued Ham with Bananas a treat not only for the palate but also for the eyes.

# Barbecued Ham with Bananas
*Vernon County Censor*, August 25, 1909[4]

Makes 4 to 6 servings

3 firm bananas

Juice of 2 lemons diluted with ½ cup water

6 slices dry-cured ham

Black pepper, to taste

1 tablespoon yellow mustard

1 tablespoon white vinegar

2 tablespoons grape or currant jelly

1 tablespoon water

Butter for greasing the cooking sheet

**Barbecued Ham with bananas**
Cut a thin slice of raw ham and after freshening in cold water dry in a towel and place in a hot frying-pan; dust it with pepper, spread sparingly with mixed mustard and pour on a tablespoonful of vinegar. Fry quickly, turning often. Remove the skins from firm bananas and after marinating them in diluted lemon-juice for thirty-minutes, cut them in halves, lengthwise, dip in softened grape or currant jelly and place on a buttered baking-sheet. Put into the oven and cook until soft, but not shapeless. Place the ham on a platter and arrange the bananas around it. Pour melted jelly over all.

Preheat oven to 400°F. Remove the peels from bananas and marinate the fruit in diluted lemon juice for 30 minutes.

Place ham slices in a hot frying pan. Dust with pepper, spread sparingly with mustard, and pour on vinegar. Fry quickly, turning often, until meat turns opaque.

Cut the bananas in half length-wise. Mix jelly with 1 tablespoon water until runny. Brush some of the mixture onto banana halves and place them onto a greased cooking sheet. Bake until soft, but not shapeless, approximately 20 minutes.

To serve, place the ham on a platter and arrange the bananas around it. Pour remaining diluted jelly over all.

# 26

## HISTORICAL CLEAN EATING

### A Spice Dilemma

Many would argue that spices were at the root of precolonial globalization. Europeans' desire to elevate their cuisine with foreign flavors—like the slow warmth of cinnamon or the pungent heat of pepper—changed the world forever. Beginning in the fifteenth century, the spice trade fueled exploration, exploitation, and political conflict, and it revolutionized the way Europeans cooked.[1] In the early trading days, spices were rare and expensive on the European market. Spiced food was a symbol of wealth and status. Eventually, however, the supply grew and costs declined, and spices had moved into kitchens of all classes by the nineteenth century. Since availability was no longer an issue, it is curious that so many of the dishes advertised in nineteenth and early twentieth century newspapers in Wisconsin are so bland. Recipes calling for a hint of peppercorn, the rare application of cayenne pepper, or the odd inclusion of paprika leave much to be desired for the contemporary gourmand.

The explanation lies within the waves of culinary trends. Similar to the more contemporary trend of "clean eating," people during the second half of the nineteenth century wanted to adopt a more "natural" way of eating. Some experts suggested that spices artificially adulterated the way foods were supposed to taste as intended by nature. An 1881 article promoting "hygienic menus," for example, suggested that readers switch to a plain, "non-stimulating," vegetarian diet, and it listed spices among unhealthy products to avoid such as alcohol, narcotics, and tobacco.[2] Advocates for this diet promised that even "the most dyspeptic glutton can cure himself in the course of a single season." And weight loss was not the only health concern addressed by the no-spice craze. Rheumatism was thought to be worsened by spicy food.[3] Additionally, those considered "Thin and Nervous" and those suffering from skin infections, such as erysipelas, were told to avoid spices, even in cakes.[4]

Bland food was also recommended as the ideal fare for children, as the *Kenosha Telegraph* printed in 1882: "Plain, good food, and plenty of it, will keep the mind and body in sound condition and supply all the requirements of growth."[5] Some nutritionists, such as John Harvey Kellogg, inventor of the famous cornflake breakfast cereal, claimed that the excitement caused by stimulating, flavorful food caused psychological damage. Kellogg was also very concerned with "masturbation insanity," and he argued that a bland vegetarian diet would help to break a vicious cycle of pubescent behaviors and an appetite for spices.[6]

The temperance movement fully supported this antispice smear campaign, claiming that children exposed to spices would ultimately turn to "degrading habits," including the consumption of alcohol: "The spices, pungents, and irritants in general, not only tend to deprave the taste, preparing the way for intemperance by producing morbid appetites, but create an unnatural thirst, a thirst which is the most naturally gratified by the use of intoxicants. Hence we shall find that boys fed in this way during the early part of life more generally become intemperate than those who have been accustomed to a more abstemious living."[7] Judging by the many recipes published in historic newspapers, the bland food craze was ubiquitous in Wisconsin and shaped seasoning habits for generations to come.

Keeping this in mind, we encourage you to take the recipes published during the antispice era with a grain of salt—quite literally, as many of the original recipes do not call for enough salt for the contemporary connoisseur. Feel free to add more and experiment with additional spices, because sometimes a taste of the past can benefit from a little spice from the present.

# Roast Beefsteak with Potato Dressing

*Wausau Pilot,* July 6, 1922[8]

Makes 6 servings

4 large potatoes, boiled and cooled

2 slices stale bread

1 tablespoon butter, plus extra for
   dotting filling

1/4 cup finely chopped onion

1/2 teaspoon salt

Black pepper, if desired

1/2 teaspoon ground sage

Cracker crumbs, if desired (see Crackers
   recipe on page 63)

3 pounds round beef steak

ROAST BEEF STEAK WITH PO-
TATO DRESSING — Select a nice
piece of round steak. Make a dressing of four large cold boiled potatoes, two slices of stale bread, half
teaspoonful of salt, tablespoon of butter, a little onion chopped fine, pepper and ground sage as liked. Put
the above ingredients in a bowl and
moisten with hot water, work with
hands until all crusts are broken up
and the materials well blended. If
the dressing seems too moist add a
small amount of cracker crumbs.
Spread on steak, dot with butter, roll
firmly and tie. Keep covered until
nearly done then uncover and let
brown. Cut in slices and serve hot.

Preheat oven to 275°F. Quarter potatoes and add to a large bowl with bread, butter, onion, salt, pepper, and sage. Moisten everything in the bowl with hot water until the bread is soft, and work with hands or potato masher until all the bread is broken up and the ingredients are well mixed. If the mixture seems too moist and won't hold together, add a small amount of cracker crumbs.

Flatten steak with a mallet or rolling pin. If steak is thick, butterfly before flattening. Spread stuffing on the meat, dot with butter, roll firmly, and tie with butcher's twine. Sear all sides in an oven-safe frying pan, cover with lid or aluminum foil, and transfer to the oven. Cook until the steak reaches an internal temperature of at least 145°F, approximately 70 minutes.

Cut in slices and serve hot.

# 27

## SHARING LOCAL RECIPES

### "The Housewife's Exchange"

Thanks to the internet and its countless food blogs and recipe sites, sharing and finding recipes today is easy. A century ago, however, a home cook looking for something new to try was limited to investing in a cookbook, exchanging recipes with friends and family members, or opening up a newspaper. As the growing news industry became increasingly connected, a press network formed in which content could be exchanged and republished.

After the turn of the twentieth century, more and more newspapers began printing syndicated recipes, which could come from anywhere in the country and were seldom credited with a location of origin. While novel, these recipes could be quite impractical for local cooks due to their dependence on regionally accessible ingredients. In an effort to combat this dilemma, the *Wausau Pilot* started The Housewife's Exchange, a column featuring recipes submitted by and for local women.[1] In addition to its goal of providing realistic and practical recipes for the local audience, the column also aimed to take the seasons into consideration. The time of year dictated not only the

## THE HOUSEWIFE'S EXCHANGE

(Send all communications to the Woman's Editor, The Pilot, Wausau.)

**In 1922, the name of the woman's editor at the *Wausau Pilot* was not publicly disclosed.**
*Wausau Pilot*, July 13, 1922

availability of ingredients but also the temperature in most kitchens, which could affect the disposition of the cook: "During the Summer months it will be sweltering in every kitchen, and knowing how women shun the heat and drudgery of meal preparation during this period, the *Pilot* has inaugurated a 'Housewife's Exchange.' "[2] Easy and fast recipes were supposed to make cooking more pleasurable in the heat, and submissions from community members were thought to be reliable, tried, and tested. Moreover, the *Pilot*, which was published on Thursdays, included a "model Sunday menu," relieving housewives of meal planning for that day.[3]

The Housewife's Exchange first appeared in June 1922 and was compiled by the woman's editor, who was likely a woman herself. Possibly due to that fact, the editor's name is never mentioned in the publication and remains a mystery. Though it lasted for just one year, the column provided Wausau readers with their neighbors' favorite recipes—including Sliced Lemon Pie, Maple Cream, Cheese Toast, Browned Parsnip, and Roast Stuffed Shoulder of Lamb—as well as the motivation to branch out and try something new.[4]

**MENU, SUNDAY, JULY 16**

**Breakfast**
Fresh Currants with Sugar
Buttered Toast         Poached Eggs
Coffee

**Dinner**
Tomato Bouillon
with Browned Potatoes
Sliced Cucumbers or Pickled Beets
Roast Stuffed Shoulder of Lamb
Lettuce Salad
Fruit Pudding
Coffee

**Supper**
Blueberry Muffins
Sliced Cold Meat
Cake         Fresh Berries
Iced Tea

**This sample menu printed in the Housewife's Exchange column offered home cooks a break from meal planning.** *Wausau Pilot*, July 13, 1922

# Roast Stuffed Shoulder of Lamb with Browned Potatoes

*Wausau Pilot,* July 13, 1922[5]

Makes 6 to 8 servings

2 cups dried bread crumbs

3 tablespoons bacon grease

1 tablespoon finely chopped onion

1 tablespoon chopped parsley

1 teaspoon salt, plus more for seasoning

½ teaspoon pepper, plus more for
  seasoning

3 ½–4 pounds lamb shoulder, deboned
  (Note: Ask your butcher to remove the
  bones but keep meat in one piece.)

1 ¼ cup water, divided

2 ½–3 pounds potatoes, boiled

1 tablespoon flour

ROAST STUFFED SHOULDER OF LAMB WITH BROWNED POTATOES —-Three and one-half to four pounds shoulder of lamb, two cups stale bread crumbs, one tablespoon finely cut onions, tablespoon drippings, one tablespoon chopped parsley, one teaspoon salt and one eighth teaspoon pepper. Wipe lamb with piece of wet cheesecloth; fill pocket with above ingredients mixed together. Sew up and put into hot over for twenty minutes. When well schred season and pour over one cup cold water and roast forty-five minutes; add one quart white potatoes, which have been washed, pared and boiled, and roast until potatoes are brown. Add more water as needed, making two cups of gravy when finished, thicken gravy by adding one tablespoon flour mixed with little cold water, season and mook until smooth.

Preheat oven to 325°F. Mix bread crumbs, bacon grease, onion, parsley, 1 teaspoon salt, and ½ teaspoon pepper in a medium bowl. Lay the meat flat and spread the mixture over it, filling the pocket where the bones were and creating an even layer of filling. Roll up the meat and tie with butcher's twine.

Sear on all sides in an oven-safe frying pan. Season with salt and pepper. Pour 1 cup of water over the meat and transfer it to the oven. Bake for 45 minutes.

Add potatoes to the pan and continue to roast until browned, about 15 minutes.

Remove the meat and potatoes from the pan. In a small dish, mix ¼ cup cold water with flour. Add the mixture to the drippings and stir until smooth. Add more water as needed to achieve desired gravy consistency. Season with salt and pepper to taste and serve with the meat and potatoes.

# FISH AND SHELLFISH

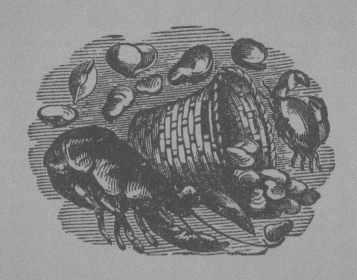

# 28

# MR. SMITH WENT FISHING LAST SATURDAY

## Life in the Social Column

The phenomenon of recounting the daily, and often mundane, aspects of our lives on a shared platform is not as exclusive to online social media as a person in the twenty-first century might think. While Aunt Becky may have posted on Facebook about visiting her brother's family last week, Mrs. Clarence Sweet of Fargo, Wisconsin, was reported to have visited her brother's family in the *River Falls Journal* in 1902.[1] Before the internet and the rise of online social media platforms, it was local newspapers that shared these daily goings-on. It was not uncommon—nay, it was rather routine—for turn-of-the-century readers to look through their Sunday paper and read, for instance, about Miss Maggie McMahon's visit with her sister in Racine or how "Mrs. E. B. Brundage entertained a large company of ladies at an afternoon tea party last Thursday, in honor of Miss Belle Brundage." In case there was any doubt, attendees of this 1890 party were reported to have had "a delightful time."[2]

These tidbits of local news often appeared in the "social column" and were as important to communities as the news stories on national and world events. While the latest reports concerning US politics or foreign affairs were certainly of interest to many readers, the social column of a newspaper often affected their lives in a more palpable way, listing functions readers could attend and mentioning people they interacted with in their community. National newspapers provided coverage of geopolitical events, but the local press offered readers updates on their neighbors.

Relics of the past, social columns now offer us a rare glimpse into the everyday lives and popular activities of Wisconsinites from long ago—as well as the occasional insight into their food culture. Where else could we learn about two couples, the Barbers and the Barstows, who went fishing on a Friday evening in 1914 and found themselves hauling "about 40 pounds of fish" on their way home?[3] Conveniently, local newspapers usually offered plenty of suggestions on how to enjoy such a catch, as well.

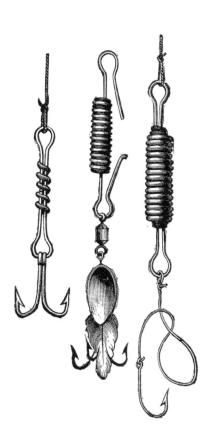

# Fish Kabab

*Wausau Pilot*, October 3, 1911[4]

Makes 4 servings

> Fish Kabab—Sharpen long straight sticks of willow or other green wood, and on them string small perch, trout or any other pan fish, alternating with thin slices of bacon or pork. Season with salt and pepper and place the laden split across forked sticks set so as to come just above a glowing bed of coals. The camp fire should be made an hour before meal time so as to insure a good bed of coals. Now keep constantly, although slowly, turning, so that the juices will not be lost in the fire. The fish will cook in a very few moments.

1 ½ pounds pan fish filets (perch, trout, or similar)

8–10 strips bacon (uncooked)

Salt and black pepper, to taste

Sharpen long, straight sticks of willow or other green wood. You can also use skewers.

Cut fish filets and bacon into 2-inch pieces. On sticks or skewers, string the fish alternating with bacon strips. Season with salt and pepper.

Hold the kebabs just above a glowing bed of coals. Turn kebabs consistently and slowly, so that the juices will not be lost in the fire. The fish will cook in a very few moments. Remove from fire when the fish is no longer translucent and flakes easily.

# WASTE NOT, WANT NOT

## Tips on Food Waste

*"What are you studying there, Clarice?"*

*"About how to make delightful dishes from left-over food. The cook has left."*

*"Well, you can make some nice dishes from left-over food."*

*"Yes; and I have plenty of material. There's a great deal of food left over since I began doing the cooking."*

*Vilas County News,* 1912[1]

Just as food waste is commonly discussed these days, it was also on the minds of nineteenth-century Wisconsinites. As early as the 1860s, Wisconsin newspapers were printing stories about the vice of "American extravagance" and encouraging readers to be mindful of how they consumed and prepared food at home.[2] Heaping food upon plates regardless of the appetite of those sitting at the table, argued one *Kenosha Telegraph* article, was bound to result in food waste and poor economy for households.[3] As the country entered World War I and certain foods began to be rationed, the US government urged citizens to do their part in decreasing food waste on the home front: "Experts in the agricultural department have estimated that the actual waste of food in the United States is $700,000,000 annually. This is in addition to the enormous consumption in excess of what is really needed to support life comfortably."[4]

Nellie Maxwell, a food journalist hailing from Wisconsin (see "Nellie Maxwell" on page 39), enthusiastically urged her readers to use leftovers in their cooking. Up until this moment in the early 1900s, the term *leftovers* had not been part of the American vernacular. However, with the arrival of ice boxes and refrigerators in the average home, Americans could now easily store food until they could use it again. This opened up new possibilities for meals. Many newspaper articles cautioned, however, that the use of leftovers should be approached in an economical manner: "When left-over food is on hand some use should be found for it which does not involve much additional material, much time for preparation, or extra fuel for cooking."[5] Readers were presented with enticing suggestions such as mixing leftover salmon into "a most appetizing salad," using leftover juice from canned fruit as a "delicious pudding sauce or as liquid in fruit cake," or drying leftover cheese to turn into cheese crumbs, which were "particularly good with starchy foods, such as potatoes, macaroni, etc."[6]

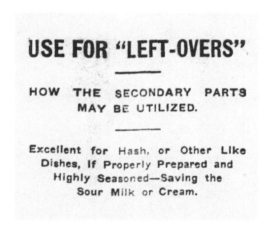

This 1915 advice about using leftovers claimed to be "just what the average American home cook needs." *Vernon County Censor*, March 31, 1915

Articles also raised the issue of leftover food's safety and provided advice to prevent spoiling before dishes could be reused and served again. "Left-over cooked foods should be kept cold and covered, used promptly, especially in warm weather, and, if possible, heated thoroughly before being served again," advised a 1924 article in the *Eagle River Review*. "Dangerous poisons sometimes develop in such foods without making noticeable changes in taste or smell."[7] The widespread availability of refrigeration in homes helped to make food storage safe and convenient, but many articles still made sure to recommend that readers unfamiliar with the new technology should "cool all left-overs before putting them away" to maintain cool temperatures and use their appliance efficiently.[8]

In 1918, an *Iron County News* article addressed "To the Women of Iron County" encouraged readers to incorporate more fish into their cooking, touting the many ways that "cooked fish left-overs" could be repurposed into an array of meals "with cream sauce, or scalloped or made into hash, croquettes, or fish-balls."[9] A recipe for fish pudding printed in *Our Land–La Nostra Terra* of Hurley in 1913 likewise presented an excellent option for using up the remnants of a fish supper. With a bit of dairy and some potatoes, an entirely new dish could be served and food waste could be avoided.

# Fish Pudding

*Our Land–La Nostra Terra,* July 5, 1913[10]

Makes 6 servings

1 pound potatoes, peeled

2 ¼ cups milk, divided

1 pound cold boiled fish

1 tablespoon flour

½ teaspoon salt

¼ teaspoon black pepper

2 tablespoon parsley, chopped

> **How to Make a Pudding.**
> Fish Pudding.—Flake one pound of cold boiled fish and place in a greased pie dish. Mix one ounce of flour, half a teaspoonful of salt and a quarter teaspoonful of pepper to a smooth paste with a little milk. Boil half a pint of milk and pour over the paste, return to the saucepan and let it boil. Add one dessertspoonful of chopped parsley and pour over the fish. Mash one pound of potatoes with a little milk and spread smoothly over fish. Ornament and place in a quick oven to brown the top.

Preheat oven to 450°F. Boil potatoes and mash them with 2 tablespoons of milk.

Flake fish and place into a greased pie dish.

In a small bowl, mix flour, salt, and pepper with 2 tablespoons of milk to make a paste.

In a saucepan, bring the remaining 2 cups milk to a boil and stir in the paste. Let simmer until the sauce thickens. Add parsley to the sauce and pour the sauce over the fish. Spread the mashed potatoes smoothly over the fish. Use a fork to create a decorative design on the top and bake until browned, about 25 minutes.

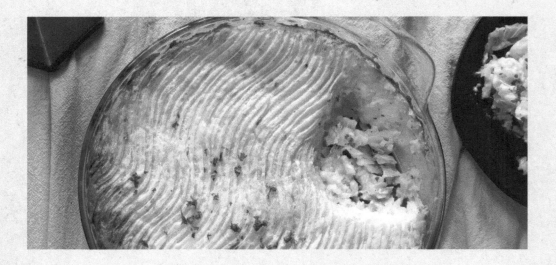

# 30

## SHIPPED ON ICE

### Lobster in the Dairy State

The lobster's reputation in colonial New England was poor. The crustacean was plentiful and cheaply found, and it was primarily eaten by the lower classes of society. Just the presence of lobster shells around one's house could be considered a mark of low economic status and a source of embarrassment.

Yet, this was not the case in Wisconsin, where people of varying social classes enjoyed lobster as early as 1850. This new market demographic was distanced from the coastal disdain for the crustaceans, and the novelty of their importation from the East Coast made them appealing to many. When the lobster arrived in Wisconsin, it was advertised as an exciting treat.

One of the first mentions of lobster being served in Wisconsin appeared in a Mineral Point Eating House advertisement in the February 1, 1850, issue of the *Wisconsin Tribune*. The restaurant announced that it would be serving "oysters, lobsters, sardines, pickled tongue pies, [and] cakes."[1] Thomas Webb & Co of Kenosha was an early importer and

**LOOK HERE.**

*JUST OPENED, on High Street, opposite*
JOHN MILTON'S STORE,
**A NEW BAKERY**
AND
**CONFECTIONERY.**

The Subscribers intend keeping constantly on hand a good supply of *Oysters, Lobsters, Sardines, Pickled Tongues, Pies, Cakes, Tarts, &c. &c., &c.*
*MEALS AT ALL HOURS.*
We have also commenced making SAUSAGE which will be sold Cheap for Cash.
1400 Lbs of Hamburgh Cheese for sale by
NASH & MARTIN,
Mineral Point Eating House.
January 23d. 1850.                    16 tf

Lobster was on the menu at the Mineral Point Eating House as early as 1850. *Wisconsin Tribune*, February 1, 1850

wholesaler of lobster to the state. Advertisements for the business's imported lobster began appearing in the mid-1850s in Kenosha's *Tribune and Telegraph*.[2]

The *Wood County Reporter* described the import of lobster and its distribution in 1889: "Seaport markets are supplied with live lobsters transported in the wells of these cruising smacks; towns a moderate distance inland are also furnished with live lobsters, while those destined for the far west are usually boiled."[3] At the time, Wisconsin would have been considered "far west" and, therefore, received lobsters preboiled and on ice. Canned lobster was also available. By the early 1900s, advances in transportation allowed for the shipment of live seafood, for the first time letting locals experience the superior taste of a freshly prepared lobster.[4]

Due to high demand and rampant overfishing, lobster has become an expensive commodity today, even in coastal locations, rebranded into a high-brow delicacy. Historical recipes, however, provide us insight into how Wisconsinites prepared it as it approached its peak in popularity.

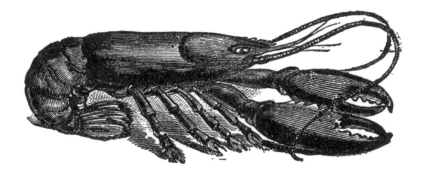

# Lobster à la Newberg

*Wausau Pilot,* November 14, 1911[5]

Makes 2 servings

1 lobster tail, fresh

1 tablespoon butter

¼ teaspoon salt

¼ teaspoon black pepper

Pinch cayenne

½ cup sherry

3 egg yolks

1 cup cream

**Lobster a La Newberg.**

One large lobster, one tablespoon butter, one gill of sherry, three eggs, half pint cream; take the nicest part of the lobster, cut in small slices, put in chafing dish with butter, season well with pepper and salt, a pinch of cayenne; pour the wine over it; cook ten minutes; add the beaten yolks of eggs and the cream; let all come to a boil and serve immediately.

Remove the shell from raw lobster tail and cut tail into bite-size slices. Add to a pan with butter. Season with salt, pepper, and cayenne. Add sherry and simmer for 10 minutes.

In a bowl, beat egg yolks with cream and add to the hot pan. Mix well. Turn up the heat slightly. As soon as it comes to a boil, remove from pot and serve hot.

# 31

# BRINY WITH A CULT FOLLOWING

## Oysters in Wisconsin

Oysters are a saltwater delicacy harvested far from the freshwater states of the Midwest. Despite Wisconsin's considerable distance from any ocean, historic newspapers confirm that the state's residents enjoyed the fresh shellfish as early as 1840. Oysters appear regularly in recipes from the 1800s, raising questions as to how fresh oysters made their way to the state before modern transportation technologies paved the way for the oyster frenzy that lasted throughout most of the nineteenth century.

Fresh, in-the-shell oysters were advertised for sale in Wisconsin as early as 1842 at a new grocery, fruit, and drug store operated by James S. Munson in Southport (later Kenosha).[1] Munson's oysters were likely from the Chesapeake Bay. Most oysters being imported to the Midwest at this time came from that area and were transported west by train.

One of the first newspaper advertisements for oysters in Wisconsin in 1842. *Southport Telegraph*, November 30, 1842

Getting oysters still in their shell all the way to Wisconsin posed a logistical challenge for nineteenth-century distributors. Oysters spoil quickly, and surely no one wanted to eat a raw oyster that was no longer fresh, even in the 1800s. To avoid

**Squire's Oyster House restaurant on Water Street in Black River Falls.** WHI IMAGE ID 42157

spoilage, oysters were packed in wooden barrels, between layers of sawdust and ice. Sawdust was commonly used for insulation in ice houses, where ice was stored for use in the summer. In the oyster barrels, sawdust fulfilled the same purpose, maintaining the low temperature of the shellfish. With Arthur Stilwell's invention of an oyster train car in the late 1800s, oysters could be transported live in tanks of saltwater and distributed across the country.[2] Because this precious cargo was so important to the public, oyster cars were often listed first in newspaper accounts of train accidents or robberies, as in this 1877 report from the *Manitowoc Pilot*: "A DIABOLICAL attempt was made on the morning of the 22d, to wreck a train on the Ohio and Mississippi road, near Noble, Ill. An oyster car, mail, express, two passenger and three sleeping coaches were thrown from the track. No lives lost."[3] As the documentation suggests, some may have considered oysters to be more important than passengers.

Today, oysters are considered an expensive luxury, especially in locations far from an ocean, but in the 1800s they were a cheap source of protein—even for Wisconsinites—and people could not seem to get enough of them. Oysters were enjoyed in the same way chicken wings or french fries are today, and they became an important fixture of Victorian nightlife. It was trendy to indulge in some oysters during a night out, and "oyster saloons" opened up around the state. One of these institutions was William Teague's, located on High Street in Mineral Point.[4] Many a pint of local beer was enjoyed there, likely with oysters on the side. Because of their low price point, oysters also became a popular ingredient in the household. From chicken and oyster pie to oyster shortcake, the mollusk was a staple of many Wisconsinites' diets in the 1800s.[5]

As with most indulgences, all good things must come to an end. The oyster craze of the Victorian era met its demise near the turn of the century. Unsustainable harvesting was depleting the number of oysters, and the public was growing concerned over unsanitary practices in the industry. Eventually, Prohibition forced the closure of many oyster saloons (which also relied on alcohol sales), pushing the oyster out of the spotlight and out of Midwestern kitchens. Despite the high price point of modern oysters, it is worth a splurge to serve them with a stewed beefsteak to get a taste of how they were enjoyed during their heyday.

# Stewed Beefsteak

*Mineral Point Tribune,* June 5, 1878[6]

Makes 4 to 6 servings

2 onions, chopped

4 pickled walnuts, chopped (see Pickled
  Walnuts recipe on page 215)

2–3 pounds rump steak

12 fresh oysters, strained

STEWED BEEFSTEAK. —Peel and chop two onions, cut into small parts four pickled walnuts, and put them at the bottom of the stewpan. See that the rump steak be cut off a proper thickness, about three quarters of an inch, and beat it flat with a rolling-pin. Place the meat on top of the onions; let it stew for an hour and a half, turning it over every twenty minutes. Ten minutes before serving up throw in a dozen oysters, with their liquor strained through a fine seive.

Add onions and pickled walnuts to a large pan.

Flatten steak with a mallet or rolling pin, then place on top of onions and walnuts in the pan.

Cover and cook on the stovetop on low for 1 ½ hours, turning the steak every 20 minutes. Add oysters to pan and let cook for 10 minutes before serving.

# SWEETS

# 32

# IN THE OLD SUGARBUSH

## Making Maple Products

A Wisconsin winter is not immediately followed by spring, but by a sweet interlude marked by fluctuating temperatures dancing around the freezing point: maple sugaring season. Long before Wisconsin established one of the largest maple-product industries in the country, Native people living in the Great Lakes region were already tapping the area's maple trees to harvest the sap. These early Native people cooked with vessels made out of wood or bark, which could not be exposed to the high heat of a direct flame but could be heated with the help of hot stones. By the time Europeans arrived, the Native populations of the Great Lakes had centuries of experience in the sugarbush. Newly arrived Euro-American settlers who wanted sweetness in their diet began learning from the sugar camp practices of their Native neighbors.[1]

One of the most important lessons European immigrants learned was that neither maple sap nor syrup keeps well for a long period of time. Lacking the luxury of modern refrigerators, some people preserved their harvest by cooking it past the syrup stage into maple sugar. In this crystallized form, the sweetener remained a staple in Native and Euro-American kitchens until the 1860s, when cane sugar became cheaper to import and the sugar beet was introduced to the area.[2] After this dip in popularity, however, maple syrup experienced a resurgence in the twentieth century. Commercial sugar bush operations in Wisconsin peaked in the 1960s when the state became home to the world's largest maple syrup–making company, Reynolds Sugar Bush, in Aniwa.[3]

The short time period early in the year—when temperatures begin to rise above freezing during the day but frost still forms at night—was crunch time for many in

**A drawing of an Ojibwe sugar camp by Seth Eastman ca. 1850.** WHI IMAGE ID 9829

northern climates attempting to produce and preserve enough sugar to last through the rest of the year. Because tapping the trees, collecting the sap, boiling the sap into syrup, and making the sugar is time consuming, maple sugaring was a social event. As nature began to signal that spring was approaching, neighbors gathered around fires in the sugarbush to work, tell stories, and celebrate the end of winter. Then, once

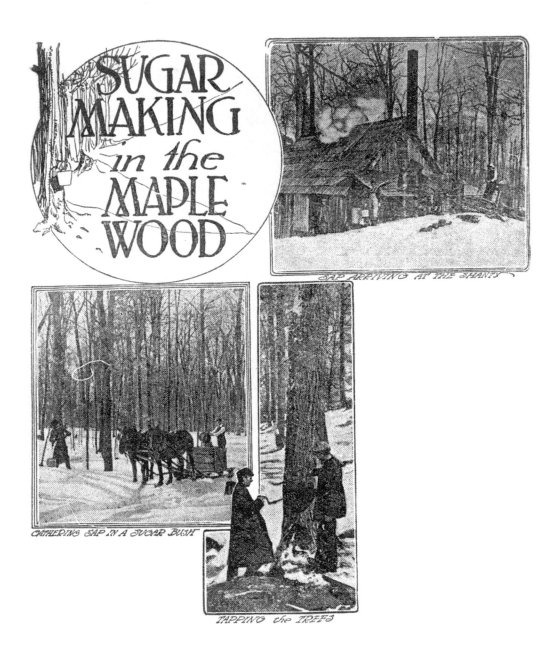

These images from the *Wauwatosa News* show various steps involved in "the art of making maple sugar." *Wauwatosa News*, March 19, 1915

enough sugar was produced, the littlest helpers were given a sweet reward: maple taffy. The *Wausau Pilot* reported on this European immigrant tradition in 1903:

The last sugaring-off at the end of the season is the day of festivities and hard work combined. The neighbors' children are there, gathered around the steaming kettle of sirup [*sic*] with their dishes and little paddles whittled out of basswood, eagerly waiting for the word when the sirup is thick enough to stir into sugar. A patch of snow is found in a sheltered spot in the woods near by and a dipperful of thick liquid is thrown over it. It quickly cools into the form of taffy. It is fine.

That night the sticky sugar is washed from hands and faces of little children, the taffy is combed out of their hair, and they are put to bed full of sweet stuff and thoughts of an enjoyable day in the old "sugar bush."[4]

Today, many Native people in the Great Lakes region continue the cultural practice of "making sugar bush," using both traditional and modern methods. In her 2013 book, *Original Local: Indigenous Foods, Stories and Recipes from the Upper Midwest*, Ojibwe writer Heid E. Erdrich explains, "Maple sugar, traditionally stored in birch-bark cones, is used to season meat, vegetables, manoomin, and berries all year long. Smoky, grainy, subtle, or strong—varied like wines—real Ojibwe maple syrup (*zhiiwaagamizigan*) or sugar cakes (*ziiga-iganan*) borrow their taste from the bark containers and the wood fires used to cook down the sap."[5] Conveniently, the following recipe for maple taffy requires just one ingredient—maple syrup—and tastes delicious whether you've made the syrup yourself or purchased it at the grocery store.

# Maple Taffy

*Wausau Pilot*, March 3, 1903[6]

Makes about 8 taffy strips

1 cup maple syrup

Find a patch of several inches of clean snow outside or freeze a metal cooking sheet outside or in the freezer.

> The last sugaring-off at the end of the season is the day of festivities and hard work combined. The neighbors' children are there, gathered around the steaming kettle of sirup with their dishes and little paddles whittled out of basswood, eagerly waiting for the word when the sirup is thick enough to stir into sugar.
>
> A patch of snow is found in a sheltered spot in the woods near by and a dipperful of thick liquid is thrown over it. It quickly cools into the form of taffy. It is fine.

Bring maple syrup to a boil. For a chewy taffy, boil the maple syrup for approximately 10 minutes. The longer the cooking time, the harder the finished taffy will be.

Slowly pour the hot syrup into the snow or onto the frozen cooking sheet in long strips. Once the syrup has cooled and hardened, remove the candy and enjoy.

# 33
# DOING WITHOUT

## Mimicking Flavors in Mock Dishes

The summer of 1910 was hot and dry in Wisconsin, especially in the northwestern part of the state. Farmers worried about their crops. The corn had already withered. There would not be much left to harvest in the fall. Producers anticipated financial losses and predicted that consumers would have to pay higher prices to secure staples. Then, finally, in mid-August, the rain came. It was the first prolonged rain that summer, and it salvaged the tobacco, sugar beets, millet grass, and buckwheat planted in the dry soil.[1] Sighs of relief could likely be heard across the state.

Historically, many factors have caused food insecurity. Failed crops and natural disasters can interfere with a harvest. Market manipulation and political conflicts can disrupt the supply chain. Often, those who are not able to afford cost increases are left with little variety in their diet. With limited options, consumers are forced to make do with what they can secure and become resourceful in creating nourishing and enjoyable meals.

Sugar beet and sugar cane shortages led Wisconsinites to use local maple sugar (see "In the Old Sugarbush" on page 138) or honey as sweetener substitutes.[2] During World War I, most US consumers were unable to purchase the amount of sugar they needed for canning. In 1919, the *Baraboo Weekly News* reported: "Baraboo merchants are not able to obtain the amounts they desire and are limiting sales to two or three pounds or more. . . . The shortage of sugar comes at a time when most housekeepers need it most. In some cities many women have been forced to give up the idea of doing much canning of fruits this year because of the shortage."[3] Although the supply of fruit was sufficient that summer, not having sugar to preserve the harvest meant it wouldn't last into the winter.

At the mercy of the seasons, and before the advent of electric refrigeration, the process of canning was as important as the crops themselves in combating food insecurity in the colder months. Hence, finding ways to use less sugar—or no sugar at all—was a recurring theme in local newspapers. One 1858 *Kenosha Tribune and Telegraph* article, for instance, introduced a method of preserving fruit without the sweetener.[4] Newspapers also printed alternative recommendations for the storage of produce, which, in some cases, could guarantee access to fresh fruit when snow eventually covered the ground.[5] Packed into barrels in a dark cellar, apples could last until they were needed for a holiday pie (see "A Historical Storage Solution" on page 82). If the harvest had been bad or the inventory had been eaten away, however, home bakers would be forced to come up with a different way to serve such sweet indulgences. Mock apple pie could be made with crackers instead of apples. Cherry pie could be re-created using cranberries and raisins or rhubarb.[6] Sour rhubarb was also a popular option for mimicking lemons in a mock lemon pie.[7] This ingenuity did not stop at pies, either. A hankering for venison could allegedly be satisfied with lamb meat that had been marinated in buttermilk or vinegar for several days.[8]

Today, we know that food insecurity is detrimental to people's physical and emotional health. The plethora of recipes for mock dishes in historic newspapers reveals not just that people have always experienced food insecurity, but also that comfort food can be incredibly important during times of want. Even when crops failed, sugar was scarce, or stored supplies had been diminished, people sought ways to pull a pie out of the oven that offered the smells and flavors of abundance.

# Mock Apple Pie

*Mineral Point Tribune*, August 11, 1887[9]

Makes 8 servings

3–4 crackers (see Crackers recipe on
page 63)

1 cup cold water

Juice of 1 lemon (about 3 tablespoons)

1 teaspoon freshly grated lemon zest

Nutmeg, to taste

1 cup sugar (regular or maple sugar)

2 pie crusts

> **MOCK APPLE PIE.**
>
> Make a paste as for apple pie. Roll
> two small crackers or break them in
> crumbs, and soak them in a cup of cold
> water while making the paste. Grate
> one lemon, or pare it very thin and cut
> this paring into the smallest pieces pos-
> sible. Add this and the juice of the
> lemon to the crackers. Flavor with nut-
> meg and stir in one cup of sugar. Cover
> a plate with paste, fill with this and set
> in the oven till partly done. Then bar
> the pie with narrow strips of paste, re-
> turn to the oven and finish baking.

Preheat oven to 350°F. Break up crackers and soak in water. Add lemon juice and
lemon zest to the crackers. Add nutmeg and stir in the sugar. Place the filling in a pie
crust and add a woven lattice top crust.

Bake for about 20 to 30 minutes until the crust is golden brown. Enjoy hot.

# 34

# A VINDICATION OF THE PRUNE

## Natural Remedies and Patent Medicine

These days, prunes have a bit of a reputation, causing some to frown upon dishes that include the dried fruit and others to completely avoid them. Yet, that was not always the case. Perhaps people of the past were just more comfortable discussing and tackling digestive issues or perhaps they simply enjoyed the taste—and convenient shelf life—of dried plums. Either way, recipes for prune dishes and remedies were not rare in the nineteenth and early twentieth century.

While taking medical advice from historical sources is not always wise, exploring them can be quite interesting. In 1919, the *Washburn Times* advised parents to give children prune juice to regulate their bowel movements, a home remedy still commonly used today: "If the child has taken prune juice, unsweetened, and orange juice occasionally the digestive tract will be in good working order."[1] The same publication praised the dried fruit as a perfect travel snack for long steamer rides, as they "can be eaten when other fruits are indigestible, and are mildly laxative. As one authority advises free use of prunes for nervous people, declaring they have a quieting effect, the eating [of] the prunes on shipboard should help to check seasickness—always augmented by 'nerves.' "[2] The *Eagle River Review* in 1923 offered a trick to enhance the prune's effect: "Add a little lemon peel to prunes while cooking. The lemon will strengthen their laxative value."[3]

Other fruits said to produce a similar effect were figs and baked apples, the former of which, in our opinion, exhibited the better marketing campaign.[4] The California

Fig Syrup Company ran advertisements with drawings of serene women who do not at all look like they are struggling with constipation—they were the face of a remedy that promised to cleanse the system and benefit the kidneys, liver, and bowels, as well as dispel "colds, headaches & fevers."[5] While these advertisements sound too good to be true, the company's Syrup of Figs product was actually one of the more harmless of the "snake oils" sold at the time.

The California Fig Syrup Co. marketed Syrup of Figs as "the only remedy of its kind ever produced." *Telegraph-Courier*, February 26, 1891

Patent medicines, or nonprescription medical remedies, became popular during the second half of the nineteenth century. Due to the lack of regulations at the time, such medicines could legally be sold as the cure for anything and contained all sorts of ingredients. For example, the "tonic and blood purifier" Peruna, which sold well into the twentieth century, primarily consisted of one active ingredient: alcohol.[6] Mrs. Winslow's Soothing Syrup, advertised as the ultimate answer to a baby's teething pain, contained morphine and tragically ended the lives of some infants.[7] Women of this time period consumed all number of tinctures, tonics, and compounds in hopes of easing their suffering from what was often referred to as "female weakness" and "female trouble." In hindsight, consuming dried fruit as natural remedies, whether they are truly effective or not, sounds much more appealing than using these questionable medications. Some fruit, like prunes, are quite tasty, and prejudices against them should not stop one from enjoying a slice of prune pie.

# Mock Pumpkin Pie

*Iron County News*, April 17, 1915[8]

Makes 8 servings

¾ pound prunes

2 eggs, well beaten

½ cup sugar

3 tablespoons butter

½ teaspoon ginger

½ teaspoon cinnamon

½ teaspoon nutmeg

Pinch salt

1 pint hot milk

1 pie crust

**Mock Pumpkin Pie.**

One cupful sifted prune pulp, two eggs well beaten, pinch salt, small piece butter about size of walnut, one-half teaspoonful each of ginger, cinnamon, nutmeg and one-half cupful sugar. If not sweet enough add more, as some prunes are not so sweet as others. One pint of milk, heated to almost boiling point. Bake with one crust like pumpkin pie. This will make two small deep pies or one large deep pie. Steam one pound prunes about three hours before sifting them.

Preheat oven to 350°F. Steam prunes in a pot with a steamer insert and some water until soft, about 10 to 15 minutes. Press prunes through a sieve or use a blender to make a smooth pulp. From this, measure out 1 cup of prune pulp and let cool.

To the cooled pulp, add eggs, sugar, butter, spices, and salt, and mix well. Stir in hot milk. Pour the mixture into a single pie crust. Do not overfill the crust as the filling will expand slightly while baking. Bake for about 30 to 40 minutes until set. Let cool before serving.

# (35)

# EATING CHOCOLATE

## A History Solidified

While the custom of drinking chocolate is quite literally ancient Mesoamerican history (see "Swiss Miss Hot Cocoa" on page 199), solid chocolate has been around for just over two centuries and originated in Europe. When Europeans first brought cacao home from their explorations, chocolate was enjoyed as a drink, and it was consumed exclusively by the rich. It was not until the 1700s, after the invention of machinery for mass production, that Europeans of lower classes were able to get their hands on the beverage and further experiment with the foreign "bean."[1]

Swiss entrepreneur François-Louis Cailler is credited with the invention, in 1819, of the first solid chocolate bar meant for eating. It was, however, rather gritty and probably not as pleasant to nibble on as modern chocolate. Six short years later, Dutch chemist Coenraad Johannes van Houten found a way to separate the rich cacao butter from the rest of the seed and treat cacao with an alkali to neutralize its natural acidity, laying the groundwork for the Dutch-processed cocoa powder available to this day.[2] After experimenting with reintroducing the extracted cacao butter to the powder and adding sugar, the Englishman Joseph Fry began pouring the now smooth mixture into a mold. In 1848, he began marketing the resulting chocolate for eating rather than drinking.[3] Nearly thirty years later, the Swiss added dairy to the mix, thereby inventing milk chocolate.

Chocolate companies existed in the United States even before the invention of solid chocolate meant for eating. However, as was the case in Europe, the term *chocolate* almost always referred to the beverage, and the companies often focused on importing

Baker's Chocolate, made by the first US chocolate company, was advertised
in the *River Falls Times* in 1897. *River Falls Times*, March 16, 1897

rather than processing. This is why chocolate can be found advertised in early Wisconsin newspapers with other imported dry goods such as coffee, spices, and indigo. The first US chocolate company was founded by the Irish chocolate maker John Hannon and a doctor from Massachusetts, Dr. James Baker.[4] It was not uncommon for medical professionals to take an interest in chocolate due to the medicinal attributes the beverage was said to have. After Hannon disappeared at sea while on chocolate import business, the company became the Baker Chocolate Company, a name still widely known in the industry today. In 1852, the same company began marketing a new type of chocolate developed by Samuel German. German's chocolate had a higher sugar content, and a century later, it inspired the layered chocolate cake with coconut and pecans often referred to as German chocolate cake, despite the fact that it's all-American.

The second half of the nineteenth century witnessed the rise of several chocolate companies on both coasts, including Ghirardelli in San Francisco in 1852 and Hershey's in Pennsylvania in 1894. The invention of eating chocolate in Europe had also caused a shift in the chocolate industry in the United States. While the large import businesses continued, the country saw a growing number of chocolatiers and candy makers who experimented with different ways to prepare eating chocolate. Chocolate for "eating, drinking, cooking, baking &c." by New York candy maker Huyler's could be found advertised in Wisconsin newspapers at the end of the century.[5] Not all chocolatiers were on the coasts, though. More locally, Wisconsinites could get their hands on delicious chocolate creations from Chicago-based candy maker Allegretti as early as 1897. By the beginning of the twentieth century, chocolate had officially completed its metamorphosis from beverage to beloved confection. Recipe developers soon followed suit, and chocolate was welcomed into home kitchens—often as an ingredient to elevate desserts like Apple de Luxe.

**The Washburn store Frost & Spies sold
Chicago-made Allegretti chocolates in 1904.**
*Washburn Times*, June 30, 1904

# *Apple de Luxe*

*Manitowoc Pilot,* November 2, 1922[6]

Makes 4 servings

## Frosting[7]

2 egg whites

1 cup powdered sugar

1 teaspoon vanilla extract

## Apples

4 baking apples of uniform size and shape

¼ cup raisins, finely chopped

¼ cup almonds, finely chopped

¼ cup pecans, finely chopped

3 ounces dark chocolate, if desired

> **Apple de Luxe.**—Chop finely three-fourths of a cupful of chopped raisins and nuts. Wash and core four tart apples of uniform size and shape. Put into a baking dish, cover with cold water and bake slowly. Do not let them lose their shape. Fill the centers with the chopped mixture and when the apples are cool cover with a powdered sugar frosting flavored with vanilla. When firm and cold coat with chocolate and we have apples Allegretti.

For frosting: Beat egg whites until soft peaks form. Fold in powdered sugar and vanilla.

For apples: Preheat oven to 300°F. Wash and core apples. Put apples into a baking dish with enough water to cover the bottom of the dish. Bake for about 45 minutes until the apples are cooked but have not lost their shape.

Mix raisins, almonds, and pecans together in a bowl. After removing apples from the oven, fill their centers with the raisin and nut mixture and let cool.

Cover the cooled apples with frosting. If desired, melt chocolate and pour over the frosting-coated apples for Apples Allegretti.

# 36

# DEATH IN RHUBARB LEAVES

## Danger in the Age of Slow Information

Whether baked into a pie, cooked into sauce, or fried into dumplings, rhubarb has been a popular spring crop since long before Wisconsin became a state. In the interest of minimizing food waste and making use of the entire plant, some turn-of-the-century cooks tried their hand at preparing the leaves as well as the stalks. In 1912, it was reported that Mrs. L. H. Palmer of Baraboo won the *Milwaukee Free Press*'s recipe contest with a trio of rhubarb dishes, including stewed leaves prepared with butter and various seasonings.[1] A similar recipe, which found its way into the The Kitchen Cabinet, praised rhubarb leaves for how well they complemented the flavor of other greens, such as spinach, sorrel, and dandelions.[2]

Today, a quick online search for rhubarb leaves will immediately result in warnings about the toxicity of the greens and cautions against their consumption. Of course, this is not a new discovery. In 1844, the *Grant County Herald* reported

### Rhubarb Greens.

Cook rhubarb leaves in just enough water to cover until perfectly tender, then drain thorougly and chop fine. Put a tablespoon of butter in the frying pan and toss the leaves in this until very hot. Season with salt, pepper and a suspicion of nutmeg, mound on a hot dish and garnish with the yolks of hard boiled eggs put through a ricer.

MRS. L. H. PALMER.
Baraboo, Wis.

A 1912 recipe for rhubarb greens, which are now commonly known to be toxic. *Baraboo Weekly News*, April 25, 1912

## POISON IN RHUBARB LEAVES

### Their Use as "Greens," Which is Sometimes Recommended, is Fraught With Grave Danger.

Do not eat the leaves of the rhubarb plant! From time to time one reads or hears advice to economize and also to freshen and purify the blood by eating green vegetables. That is all right with certain important limitations, and one of these limitations concerns the leaves of the rhubarb plant. Green vegetables have a very valuable place in the food schedule, and boiled "greens," such as cabbage, kale, turnip tops and beet tops are wholesome. The eating of turnip tops and beet tops has led to the assumption that rhubarb tops are good.

That is not the fact. There is a danger sign on them. Men have been poisoned by eating them. They contain oxalic acid and death lurks in that acid.

A fatal case of poisoning by rhubarb leaves was reported some time ago in the New York Medical Journal.

The red and rosy stalk of the rhubarb has been proved by generations of cooks and generations of men and women at table to be a wholesome and palatable food. It is good as sauce and as filling for pie. But the green foliage of the plant should not be used as "greens."

This 1921 caution against eating rhubarb leaves mentions a fatal case of poisoning reported in the *New York Medical Journal*. *Washburn Times*, July 28, 1921

that an East Coast family was poisoned. Scientists soon determined that this was due to the high concentration of oxalic acid in rhubarb leaves. The medical community was gaining an understanding, even if rudimentary, of the danger of the plant. Reporting on the tragic family poisoning, the article concluded, "Every day adds to the utility of the science of vegetable chemistry, by bringing forward new discoveries in the uses of the different parts of plants."[3] While this knowledge may have caught on in the scientific community, it was inconsistently passed on among average American households, and accidental poisonings continued to occur in kitchens across the country.

In 1876, a servant outside of Minneapolis prepared rhubarb greens in an attempt to follow dietary advice that had been given to her employer. The whole Schutte family, as well as their farm hand Fred Rolf, fell ill shortly after the meal. Three and a half hours later, Rolf, who had eaten the largest portion of all, was dead. In an article titled "Death in Rhubarb Leaves," the *River Falls Journal* reported, "The case is especially sad, as Rolf's family, on the way from Germany, reached Corcoran on Friday, just in time to see their son and brother a corpse."[4]

Seven years later, authorities assumed that a four-year-old girl from Palmyra, Wisconsin, had been poisoned by rhubarb leaves she had ingested while playing outside.[5] In 1886, along with another case of rhubarb-leaf poisoning, the *Mineral Point Tribune* reported that a family fell ill after eating rhubarb sauce. Medical professionals explained the illness as having been caused by a toxic chemical reaction involving the acid found in the stalks and the metal of the cooking vessel.[6] Due to the potential for such chemical reactions, it is recommended that even nontoxic rhubarb stalks be cooked in stainless steel or enameled cookware.

Decades after the first rhubarb-leaf poisoning cases were reported in the local press, newspapers continued to print recipes including toxic rhubarb greens, illustrating how much we benefit from the shift in information-sharing pathways today. Without easy access to books on botany or other scientific sources, people relied on communal knowledge and personal experiences. Kitchen notes were sometimes passed on through generations, functioning as reference texts for cooking and home gardening. However, if no one in the community had learned about the toxicity of rhubarb greens, the imminent danger may not have been recorded. Furthermore, if a trustworthy institution like a local newspaper printed a delicious-sounding recipe, many readers likely found no reason to doubt its safety.

Centralized agencies such as the US Department of Agriculture, fueled by the dangerous misinformation that they saw being spread "in certain newspapers and magazines," eventually started launching consumer safety campaigns warning people about common toxins. A 1917 article based on USDA information and printed in the *Baraboo Weekly News* cautioned: "Because rhubarb leaves contain certain substances which make them poisonous to a great many persons, specialists of the United States department of agriculture warn housewives against using this portion of the plant for food."[7] As opposed to sporadic articles that alerted readers to poison cases, large campaigns could spread information with authority and much more widely and frequently. As a result, rhubarb greens were eventually eradicated from ingredient lists. Now, with this knowledge at our fingertips, we can carry on eating just the stalks—in moderation, of course.

# Rhubarb Tartlets

*Kenosha Telegraph*, July 16, 1880[8]
Makes 4 servings

## Crust

3 egg yolks

1 egg white

1 ¼ cups flour

2 tablespoons sugar

2 tablespoons cold butter, flaked

Pinch salt

## Filling

4 cups chopped rhubarb

½ cup water

½ cup sugar

1 tablespoon lemon juice

Whipped cream to serve

RHUBARB TARTLETS.—Make a short paste with one white and three yelks of eggs, one ounce of sugar, one ounce of butter, a pinch of salt, and flour quantity sufficient; work it lightly, roll it out to the thickness of a quarter of an inch. Line some patty-pans with it, fill them with uncooked rice to keep their shape, and bake them in a moderate oven till done. Remove the rice, and fill the tartlets with rhubarb, stewed with plenty of sugar and a dish of lemon-juice, and at the top put a heaped spoonful of whipped cream.

Preheat oven to 350°F.

For crust: Combine egg yolks, egg white, flour, sugar, butter, and salt in a medium bowl. Mix lightly and roll out to the thickness of a quarter of an inch. Line four 4-inch tart pans with the crust and dock with a fork to prevent air pockets. Fill with uncooked rice or pie weights and bake until golden brown, approximately 25 minutes. Remove the rice/weights and let crust cool.

For filling: In a pot (preferably stainless steel or enameled), stew rhubarb with water, sugar, and lemon juice. Once the rhubarb has cooked down fully, pour the mixture into the tartlet crusts and let cool.

To serve, top the tartlets with a heaping spoonful of whipped cream.

# 37

# GERMAN-LANGUAGE RECIPES

## A Tale of Culinary Integration

While the majority of Wisconsin's nineteenth-century newspapers were printed in English, more foreign-language publications began to emerge as immigrant communities grew throughout the latter half of the century. The second most popular printed language during that time was German, with more than two hundred newspaper titles published in the language across the state.[1] Like their English counterparts, German-language newspapers also included recipes. The dishes found in these recipe columns, however, were not always representative of the German immigrants' cultural background.

While some newspapers did include instructions for how to make a good schnitzel and a traditional loaf of pumpernickel, some published recipes that reflected changes the immigrants were making as they adapted to their new culinary landscape. The *Nord Stern* of La Crosse, for example, printed a recipe for "Indian Pudding" made with cornmeal, an ingredient not traditionally found in the German kitchen.[2] The array of recipes in German-language newspapers from this time period reveals that German American food culture has been profoundly shaped by assimilation and integration. German Americans, like other immigrants, often performed a balancing act to simultaneously conform and hold onto not just their native language and traditions but also their food.

While most immigrants likely brought recipes from their homelands to the United States, those dishes may have been difficult or impossible to cook in the new land if familiar ingredients were too costly or not available at all. A new environment could affect more than just the flavor of traditional dishes. Due to the arbitrariness of measurements (see "Measurements and Standardization" on page 50) used in the United States at the time, many German dishes got lost not only in translation but also in conversion. Germany, like the United States, had not adopted the standardized metric system by the time many Germans crossed the Atlantic. Until 1872, the units used to measure ingredients in Germany differed depending on the kingdom, duchy, or principality. Immigrants were lucky if their families had brought over the nonstandard heirloom cups or spoons that had been used for generations to make traditional recipes. However, if those recipes were then passed on to a friend or submitted to a newspaper in the United States, continuing the cooking tradition suddenly involved a lot of guesswork.

To make matters worse, seemingly standardized measurements, such as the pound referred to in some recipes, could actually be interpreted in many different ways. If the recipe had been adapted to fit the customary US measurement system, 1 pound roughly equaled 453.6 grams, but the recipe could have been written using the German standard pound, introduced in 1858, in which 1 pound equaled 500 grams, or any of the more localized weight definitions used throughout Germany.

Without a doubt, recipes have the best chance of being passed down over generations if they include ratios. For example, the instruction to use one part flour to one part water for a boiled pancake leaves little room for confusion.[3] Still, this practice was rare. The German-language recipes being published in different parts of Wisconsin at the time include a range of different measurements. A 1900 Zwiebelkuchen (onion cake) was made with 1 tablespoon of flour and half a pint of sour cream, while a 1912 Italian pancake called for 40 grams of flour and 1.25 liters of water.[4] Over time, however, most recipes in German-language newspapers came to reflect the standardized US measurement system, showing that many German immigrants had found a way to assimilate while preserving their culinary traditions. A new German American culinary culture was born.

# Swimming Island

*Der Sonntagsbote*, December 4, 1910[5]

Makes 1 serving

1 hard-boiled egg

⅓ cup plus 1 tablespoon sugar, divided

2 tablespoons cinnamon

1 egg

6 tablespoons flour

2 tablespoons milk

Oil, for deep frying

1 cup red wine

Rezepte zum Küchenzettel.

Schwimmende Insel. — Ein Ei wird hart gekocht, abgeschält und in Zucker und Zimt gewälzt. Nun macht man von einem Ei und Mehl einen nicht zu dünnen Pfannkuchenteig, taucht das Ei hinein und bäckt es in heißer Butter und Fett schwimmend schön goldbraun. Dann wälzt man es wieder in Zucker und Zimt, bäckt es wieder schwimmend, und so fort, bis der Teig aufgebraucht ist. Zuletzt legt man es auf eine Schüssel und übergießt es mit versüßtem heißen Wein.

Peel hard-boiled egg and toss in a bowl with ⅓ cup sugar and cinnamon.

Make a not-too-thin pancake batter by combining the egg, flour, and milk. Dip the sugared egg into the batter. Heat oil (2–3 inches deep) in a pan over medium-high heat, and deep fry the battered egg until golden brown. Remove from oil and toss again in sugar and cinnamon. Dunk it again in the pancake batter and fry. Repeat three times total.

In a separate saucepan, heat wine with remaining 1 tablespoon sugar and stir until dissolved.

To serve, place the egg in a bowl and douse it with the sweetened hot wine.

# 38

## DOOR COUNTY CHERRIES

### An Explosive Success Story

"In this one county, projecting out into Lake Michigan, several thousand acres of cherry orchards thrive. And Door County cherries are justly famous," proclaimed the *Iowa County Democrat* in 1919.[1] Though Door County had become famous for its fruit production by the early 1900s, the area's limestone-laden terrain proved a challenge to its European immigrant inhabitants in the early nineteenth century. Crops like wheat and potatoes, which were traditionally grown by Wisconsin's immigrant populations, failed in the environment. It wasn't until the late 1860s that Swiss-born Joseph Zettel found success in planting apple trees in Door County. The shallow, rock-filled soil provided ample drainage for the fruit trees, and Lake Michigan and Green Bay added environmental protection against frost and other harsh weather conditions. Building on the success of Zettel's apple trees, University of Wisconsin horticulture professor E. S. Goff and Wisconsin fruit grower A. L. Hatch joined forces in the late nineteenth century to experiment with other fruits in Door County. In 1896, the duo planted tart cherries, the Montmorency variety, north of Sturgeon Bay, and the fruit soon began to flourish.

Farmers in Door County witnessed Hatch and Goff's success and began planting their own orchards. Though the cherries thrived in the county's climate, challenges still remained, including the fact that the bedrock was "but a few inches below the surface in many places."[2] It was reported that some farmers resorted to dynamite to break up the ground for planting on their acres.[3] To manage the bulk of the harvest, orchard owners started hosting cherry-picking camps. These were advertised as a

**A postcard of tourists picking cherries in Door County, ca. 1920.** WHI IMAGE ID 112505

wholesome summer activity for both boys and girls. In the early twentieth century, between four and five thousand school-aged children would spend four to five weeks of their summers in the orchards.[4] In the 1920s, this practice came under criticism from both politicians and the public as concerns about child labor grew. Growers also hired American Indian migrant pickers from the neighboring Oneida, Lac du Flambeau, and Menominee reservations to help with their cherry harvests in the early decades of the century. By midcentury, with the industry booming and a wartime labor shortage, orchard owners brought migrant workers from the US South and Southwest, Mexico, Jamaica, and the Bahamas to pick their crops[5]

As demand for the area's cherries grew, farmers began formulating plans to promote the industry as a tourist attraction. In support of this endeavor, the state expedited the extension of a highway into Door County "in time for the tourist travel to the cherry orchards."[6] Advertisements highlighted the beautiful cherry blossom season and pick-your-own orchard experiences to entice visitors to the area. Tourists traveling home from Door County with buckets full of cherries had nearly endless possibilities for what to make with the fruits of their labor. If any cherries survived the snacking that surely took place during the drive home, then perhaps a pie, fritter, or cherry-topped sundae would make an appearance on the table.

# *Cherry Fritters*

*Wisconsin Weekly Blade*, July 20, 1916[7]

Makes 10 fritters

1 cup pitted cherries

½ cup sugar

1 cup flour

1 teaspoon baking powder

¼ teaspoon salt

2 eggs

½ cup milk

1 tablespoon butter, melted

Oil, for frying

Syrup, if desired

Powdered sugar, if desired

**Cherry Fritters.**

Sift together one cupful of flour, one teaspoonful of baking powder and one-fourth teaspoonful of salt. Add to one-half cupful of milk two well beaten eggs, a level tablespoonful of melted butter and, lastly, the dry ingredients. Now add one cupful of pitted cherries which have been mixed with one-half cupful of granulated sugar, stir thoroughly, then drop by spoonfuls into deep fat and fry as ordinary fritters. Serve hot with sirup.

Mix cherries and sugar. In a medium bowl, mix flour, baking powder, and salt. In a separate bowl, beat eggs with milk and butter. Add the wet ingredients to the dry and mix until combined. Thoroughly stir in the sugar-coated cherries.

In a pot, heat oil (2–3 inches deep). Drop the dough by the spoonful into the hot oil and deep fry each side until golden brown.

Serve with syrup or powdered sugar, if desired

# EARLY WISCONSIN APICULTURE

## Historical Beekeeping Tips

Beekeepers know that the act of maintaining bee colonies is much more complicated than many believe, even with centuries' worth of information at their fingertips. Beekeeping equipment has not changed much since the invention of the movable frame beehive, patented by New Englander Lorenzo Langstroth in 1852.[1] Previously, many

apiarists had kept their bees in the more traditional skep beehives—the upside-down baskets often associated with traditional beekeeping and Winnie the Pooh. Unfortunately, it was nearly impossible for early beekeepers with skep hives to inspect a colony for diseases or extract honey, often done by pressing the entire skep until honey came out, without destroying the hive and killing many bees. "At its best," stated a 1908 article in the *Wauwatosa News*, "this pressed honey…was often contaminated with juices of crushed larvae and other impurities."[2] Langstroth's alternative offered beekeepers a less invasive and cleaner way to foster their bees' well-being and harvest honey for human consumption. In the movable frame beehive, bees built their combs inside a box on wooden frames that could be removed individually for

**A 1914 depiction of an apiary using movable frame beehives.** *Wausau Pilot*, July 7, 1914

inspection or harvest and then returned without harming the insects. This revolutionary invention is still the most common beehive used today.

Despite advances in technology, one of the trickiest challenges for beekeepers remains the winter season. Honeybees are not native to North America and were brought over from Europe in the seventeenth century, but they are quite capable of surviving the harsh temperatures of Wisconsin winters. They stay warm by forming clusters in which they create heat through small muscle movements and rotate positions to keep one another warm. Hence, as one 1877 beekeeper warned, it's "not extreme cold weather that causes bees to perish, but a sudden change and a continuation of cold."[3] During extremely long winters, bees can run out of honey and starve. Early mild temperatures can confuse bees into thinking it's spring, causing them to become more active and use up more resources, which then leads them to suffer during another freeze. Turn-of-the-century Wisconsin newspapers were filled with tips on how to help the insects through the coldest time of the year, including this advice: "To keep bees in the winter[,] the hive must be under shelter and protected against the cold. At the same time the hive must not be kept too warm, as the bees give off considerable animal heat in the hive, and may thus be tempted to come out should the weather be moderate, perishing with cold before they can return. Enough honey should be left in the hive to supply them until spring."[4]

Of course, bees are not the only ones interested in a honey supply during the cold winter months. To combat mice, early experts suggested "partially closing the fly-hole" that critters could squeeze through.[5] To keep bears and other large predators at bay, some advised placing the hive in a "cellar or house built exclusively for that purpose."[6] Finally, "when the proper season rolls around," readers were encouraged to "put [the bees] up immediately after they have flown out, or in a few days, and leave them undisturbed in midnight darkness, and all will be right in the spring."[7] All would be right, that is, if no parasites or diseases had befallen the colony. Luckily, beekeepers throughout history have not been entirely discouraged by the amount of advice thrown their way. All the work and care that goes into apiculture continues to pay off, not just in the form of sweet golden honey but also in all the flowers, fruit, and vegetables that thrive thanks to these industrious pollinators.

# Honey Cookies

*Wauwatosa News*, September 13, 1918[8]

Makes about 20 cookies

3 cups flour

1 ½ teaspoons ground cinnamon

1 teaspoon ground cloves

1 teaspoon ground allspice

½ teaspoon salt

½ teaspoon baking soda

1 egg

⅔ cup honey

⅔ cup sugar

¼ pound walnuts, finely chopped

2 ounces finely chopped candied orange peel (see Candied Orange Peel recipe on page 185)

Preheat oven to 375°F. Sift together flour, spices, salt, and baking soda.

In a separate bowl, beat egg and add it to the dry ingredients along with honey and sugar. Stir in nuts and orange peel. Knead thoroughly, roll out thin, and cut with a biscuit cutter.

Bake for 10 minutes.

Note: These cookies are quite hard but perfect to dunk into tea or coffee.

**Honey Cookies.**

2-3 cupful honey
2-3 cupful sugar
2¼ cupfuls flour
½ teaspoonful soda
1½ teaspoonfuls cinnamon
1 teaspoonful cloves
½ teaspoonful salt
1 teaspoonful allspice
2 ounces finely chopped candied orange peel
¼ pound walnut meats, finely chopped

Sift together the flour, spices, and soda, and add other ingredients. Knead thoroughly roll out thin, and cut with a biscuit cutter. These cookies are very hard.

For other recipes send to the United States department of agriculture for Farmers' Bulletin No. 653, "Honey and Its Uses in the Home."

Make the most of your honey supply and save the sugar.

# COCO(A)NUTS

## A Taste from Far-Away Lands

The coconut is not exactly an ingredient one expects to find in nineteenth-century Wisconsin recipes. Despite needing to be imported from far away and shipped across the country, the fruit of the coconut palm tree actually appeared quite frequently in local newspapers. It was, however, usually spelled *cocoanut*. The letter *a* was dropped in the twentieth century, likely to combat any confusion with cocoa, the main ingredient in chocolate.

The coconut is not native to the continental United States. According to an 1886 article, the coconuts then available for purchase in the United States were imported from South Pacific islands, including Samoa, Tonga, and Fiji, as well as from the West Indies and Central and South America, where coconuts had been cultivated since colonial times.[1]

Historically, coconuts have served an array of purposes. Coir, the fibers found in the husk, are used to make ropes and nets. Young green coconuts can be picked from the tree and cut open to provide refreshing coconut water. Nineteenth-century consumers in the continental United States, however, likely never got a taste of this beverage because shipping routes were simply too long. Once matured, a coconut will turn brown and fall off the palm tree, at which point it has more meat, which can be eaten, but less water.

The majority of the coconuts that arrived in the United States from the South Pacific were shipped to San Francisco as copra, "the broken or crushed meat of the cocoanut, sun-dried for shipment."[2] In San Francisco, oil crushers extracted the coconut oil for

# A Nut-Made Butter

## Made From Cocoanuts at the Price of ANIMAL FAT-MADE Oleomargarine

This is to users of oleomargarine. Also to butter users who rebel at butter's cost. Some Old-World scientists have solved the problem of making butter out of cocoanuts. Think of that. It is made entirely from that delicious nut-meat which you use in shredded form on cake.

It is churned with milk to give it butter flavor. A capsule of butter color comes in every carton. So it looks and tastes like butter of the finest grade. But this vegetable fat all comes from Tropic cocoanuts.

### The Name Is Troco

This product is called Troco. It is made in Milwaukee by the Troco Nut Butter Company, in a model modern creamery.

We use the identical process which is used in Europe, where this new delicacy was created.

Any grocer will supply it to you under this guarantee:

*"If one pound of Troco fails to prove itself the best article you ever tasted in place of butter, we will gladly return your money."*

### Made from Cocoanuts

The usual oleomargarine is made, as you know, from beef fat, hog fat and often cotton seed oil. It is churned with milk, as Troco is, to give it butter flavor.

It is a cleanly, healthful product. But lard and oleo and cotton seed oil seem uninviting spreads. That's why so many cling to butter, despite the butter cost.

But Troco comes from the white meat of the cocoanut. No food in the world is more appealing.

It has the same food value as butter. It looks and tastes like butter. And you rarely find a butter so pure and sweet as Troco.

### Greater Economy

Troco costs about the same as high-grade oleomargarine. Its use will save you much, as compared with butter at the average price.

You sacrifice nothing whatever. You get no lard, no oleo in it. You get no cotton seed oil You get nothing but the fat of the cocoanut, churned with milk and salted.

For your own sake, try one pound It will be a revelation. If you are not delighted, get your money back.

___

*Notice:* Under the law, all butter substitutes must be branded Oleomargarine. That law was passed before Troco was invented. So the Troco package is branded "Oleomargarine" though there is no oleo in it.

All butter substitutes must also pay an extra tax if colored. So the color for Troco comes in a capsule. Add it yourself, as you do with oleomargarine.

**BEGIN NOW** Order a pound or two of Troco today. Your dealer has it, or can get it easily. Put Troco to a competitive test. Both your palate and your pocketbook will decide in favor of Troco. If you are not pleased, your money back.

## TROCO NUT BUTTER COMPANY, Milwaukee, Wis.

Milwaukee's Troco Nut Butter Company advertised in Eagle River's *Vilas County News* in 1917. *Vilas County News,* September 26, 1917

consumption and further processing into products such as soap and butter alternatives. The coconuts harvested in Central and South America and the West Indies, on the other hand, were shipped whole to New Orleans, and many made their way up the Mississippi River. By 1885, over two million coconuts arrived in St. Louis, Missouri, every year to be cracked, shredded, and dried for consumption as desiccated coconut.[3]

Because of this flourishing import business, coconuts and coconut products were readily available at local grocers, even in Wisconsin. In 1846, for instance, a Mr. Boone advertised his cocoanut cakes in the *Southport Telegraph*.[4] In Superior in 1871, desiccated cocoanut was available for purchase at H. B. Hill's store, and by the early twentieth century, cocoanut butter—often sold with a capsule of butter-colored dye—was advertised as a cheap alternative to the dairy variety.[5] The frequency of advertisements for, and recipes including, coconuts captures the popularity of the fruit throughout the state, as well as Wisconsinites' eagerness to make it shine.[6]

# Cocoanut Cake

*Wood County Reporter*, July 12, 1888[7]

Makes about 10 servings

## Cake

½ cup butter

1 cup sugar

2 eggs

⅔ cup milk

1 teaspoon vanilla extract

2 cups flour

2 teaspoons baking powder

Pinch salt

> **COCOANUT CAKE.**
> One tablespoonful of butter and one cup of sugar, rubbed to a cream; two-thirds of a cup of milk, two eggs, two cups of flour, two teaspoonfuls of baking powder. Ice the top with the whites of two eggs beaten with powdered sugar and grated cocoanut.

## Frosting

2 egg whites

1 cup powdered sugar

1 cup shredded coconut (plus more for decorating)

Note: Double this recipe if making a multilayer cake.

For cake: Preheat oven to 350°F. Cream together butter and sugar, then add eggs, milk, and vanilla, and mix well.

In a separate bowl, combine flour, baking powder, and salt. Add the dry ingredients to the wet. Mix until combined and pour into a greased 9-inch cake pan or springform pan.

Bake until golden brown and an inserted toothpick comes out clean, about 30 minutes. Let cool.

For frosting: Whip egg whites until they form soft peaks. Slowly add powdered sugar. Fold in 1 cup coconut.

Remove cake from pan and cover with frosting. Or, if desired, carefully cut the cake into two or three layers and spread the frosting between each layer and on top of the cake. Decorate top of frosted cake with additional shredded coconut.

# 41

# COTTAGE CHEESE PROPAGANDA

## Nellie Hatch's Rationing Recipes

In 1918, the nation was in the throes of World War I. The US Department of Agriculture (USDA) was looking for ways to support the home front and send necessary food to troops overseas. One major effort toward this goal was rationing: if Americans could ration meat and wheat products, these items could be sent to the troops in Europe. President Woodrow Wilson introduced "Meatless Monday" and "Wheatless Wednesday"—initiatives meant to encourage Americans to voluntarily partake in the nation's rationing goals. As part of these rationing campaigns, citizens were introduced to nourishing alternatives to meat and wheat, with the star of the show being cottage cheese.

As meal plans promoting meatless and wheatless recipes started appearing in Wisconsin's newspapers, so did recipes featuring cottage cheese as an excellent meat substitute. By 1918, cottage cheese was mentioned in Wisconsin's newspapers almost three times as often as it had been just four years earlier. Some articles praised cottage cheese as an easily produced source of protein , like this one in the *Watertown News*: "A pound of cottage cheese contains as much protein as 1 ½ lbs. pork chops. It contains more protein than meat [and it] is as valuable a food as meat."[1] The *Northern Wisconsin Advertiser* also lauded cottage cheese as an inexpensive meat substitute: "It contains a larger percentage of protein (the chief material for bodybuilding) than most meats and furnishes this material at a lower cost."[2]

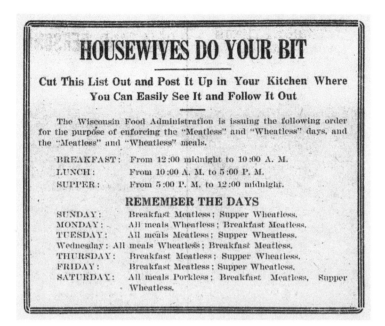

# HOUSEWIVES DO YOUR BIT

### Cut This List Out and Post It Up in Your Kitchen Where You Can Easily See It and Follow It Out

The Wisconsin Food Administration is issuing the following order for the purpose of enforcing the "Meatless" and "Wheatless" days, and the "Meatless" and "Wheatless" meals.

BREAKFAST:   From 12:00 midnight to 10:00 A. M.
LUNCH:   From 10:00 A. M. to 5:00 P. M.
SUPPER:   From 5:00 P. M. to 12:00 midnight.

### REMEMBER THE DAYS

SUNDAY:   Breakfast Meatless; Supper Wheatless.
MONDAY:   All meals Wheatless; Breakfast Meatless.
TUESDAY:   All meals Meatless; Supper Wheatless.
Wednesday: All meals Wheatless; Breakfast Meatless.
THURSDAY:   Breakfast Meatless; Supper Wheatless.
FRIDAY:   Breakfast Meatless; Supper Wheatless.
SATURDAY:   All meals Porkless; Breakfast Meatless, Supper Wheatless.

In 1918, the Wisconsin Food Administration disseminated the following notice about "Meatless" and "Wheatless" days.
*Ladysmith News-Budget*, March 1, 1918

Such articles, most often published by the Wisconsin Food Administration in conjunction with the USDA, intentionally garnered interest in cottage cheese in the hopes that the dairy product would replace a portion of meat consumption in the state's households. To instruct families on how to utilize cottage cheese in recipes, the economics department of the University of Wisconsin worked with the USDA to hire a spokesperson, Nellie Hatch of Green Bay. In this position, Hatch visited communities across the state to discuss and demonstrate the uses and advantages of the curdled milk product. Newspapers reported on her events and printed the various recipes she demonstrated to share with readers.

Whether cottage cheese truly strengthened America's home front during World War I is debatable. However, Hatch and her cottage cheese promotional tour have left us with an interesting collection of innovative recipes. Her "Cottage Cheese Salad Dressing" and "Cottage Cheese Sundae," for example, are recipes that might not exist if not for the rationing initiatives of World War I.[3] Next time you see cottage cheese in a salad bar, think of Hatch and the important role cottage cheese once played in American history.

# Cottage Cheese Sundae

*Iowa County Democrat*, November 21, 1918[4]

Makes 6 servings

2 cups cottage cheese

2 tablespoons cream

1 tablespoon sugar (or 1 ½ tablespoons corn syrup)

Chopped nuts, if desired

Chopped fruit, if desired

Jam or fruit preserves, if desired

> Cottage cheese sundae—Mix two cupfuls of cottage cheese with two tablespoonfuls cream, one tablespoonful sugar or one and one-half tablespoonfuls corn sirup, a few chopped nuts or any desired fruits you may have on hand. Put a generous spoonful in individual dessert dishes and pour jam or preserves on each helping.

Mix cottage cheese with cream and sugar (or corn syrup). Stir in chopped nuts and any desired fruits. Put a generous spoonful into 6 individual dessert dishes and, if desired, pour jam or preserves on each helping.

# 42
## A HISTORY OF CANDY
### From Medicine to Sweet Indulgence

November 16, 1901, was an exciting day in Wisconsin Rapids—a town still known as Grand Rapids at the time. It was Saturday, and a jubilant crowd of residents gathered to take a peek at a candy store that was opening its doors for the first time.[1] The proprietor, described by the *Wood County Reporter* as "confectionary and candy man" George Akins, designed his candy kitchen to be the answer to a local yearning for sweets "from plain to every description of fancy."[2] At the turn of the century, Halloween had not yet become a sugary affair, so it was the weeks leading up to Christmas and the end of the year during which people especially liked to indulge in confections. Customers ordered in advance to make sure they could present their families with scrumptious treats for the holidays.

According to advertisements from this era, most candy stores, including Akin's, offered a large

**Akin's Candy Kitchen**

We are specially prepared to furnish schools and churches with pure Home Made Candies at very low rates for the Xmas and New Year holidays.

**Geo. Akins,** PROP.

At the "WHITE FRONT"

Grand Rapids,        East Side.

Akin's Candy Kitchen in Grand Rapids (now Wisconsin Rapids) ran this ad in the *Wood County Reporter* on December 26, 1901. *Wood County Reporter,* December 26, 1901

variety of sweets. Although the exact types are seldom listed in detail, stores commonly mentioned taffy, peanut candy, chocolates, bonbons, fudge, caramels, and butterscotch. Besides candy, many confectioners also sold seasonal fruits, suggesting that these were considered more of an indulgence than a commodity to be picked up with the rest of the groceries. This has obviously changed since the advent of the grocery store (see "Carry Your Own Basket!" on page 186). Fruit is no longer sold at the candy store, sugary products can easily be found alongside other groceries, and independent candy makers have become relatively rare businesses. Although it may seem like confectionery stores have been around forever, they were actually a fairly new line of business in the Progressive Era.

For a long time, Americans did not indulge in candy but rather consumed it for medicinal purposes. Candies were marketed as cures for ailments, such as sore throats and bowel issues, and sold by apothecaries as part of their supply of patent medicine (see "A Vindication of the Prune" on page 146). It was not until the nineteenth century that the first candy stores started to appear. A look at Americans' sugar consumption

In this 1904 ad, Cascarets were marketed as "candy medicine."
*Mineral Point Tribune*, December 31, 1903

during the decades around the turn of the century suggests that by the 1880s, people had gone from consuming sugar for health reasons to noshing on sweets for pleasure. While the average person consumed 47.6 pounds of sugar between 1881 and 1885, that number nearly doubled to 86.1 pounds per capita between 1911 and 1915.[3]

As the nation developed a sweet tooth, it also created rules around the act of indulging in sweets among company. In 1922, the *Wisconsin Weekly Blade* of Madison printed an article outlining candy etiquette: "There is really a very nicely balanced table of etiquette concerning candy. Of course, the keynote of it is not to be greedy and not to be selfish—that is, not to be greedy if the candy belongs to somebody else, and not to be selfish if it is yours."[4] According to the article, a guest may accept a host's offer of one piece of candy but should take just one or two more after that to avoid being labeled as rude. One in possession of candy, on the other hand, should always share it and never dare to keep it to themselves. These rules were probably just as hard for Wisconsinites to follow a century ago as they are for us today.

# Candied Orange Peel

*Watertown Weekly Leader,* February 13, 1914[5]

Makes 2 to 3 cups

3 oranges

Pinch salt

1 cup white sugar (plus more for
tossing)

Peel the oranges and cut the peels into
¼-inch thick slices. Place the peels in
boiling water. After a minute, pour out the
water. Repeat this cycle with fresh water
3 times to remove the bitter taste.
Then, boil the peels in water with salt
until tender, about 15 to 20 minutes.

**Candied Orange Peel.**—Take the halves of oranges or grape fruit left from the breakfast table, throw them in cold water and let stand until you have a sufficient quantity, then put them into boiling water and scald, pouring off the water, adding fresh water three times to remove the bitter taste. Then scrape out the white inner pulp and put the yellow skins back into the water; add salt and cook until tender; cut in thin strips and boil in a heavy sirup until all the sugar is absorbed. Lay on plates to dry.

This confection may be used for any number of dishes, as a garnish for a dish of orange ice or ice cream it is especially nice, and may also add to the appearance of the dish if nicely arranged.

Mix sugar with 2 cups of fresh water in a pot, add orange peel and bring to a boil.
Stir and boil until the liquid is absorbed. Remove peels from pot and lay on plates to
dry for several hours. While the peels are still sticky, toss them in sugar. This adds
to the appearance, as well as the taste, of the peels.

# 43

## CARRY YOUR OWN BASKET!

### The Revolution of the Grocery Store

Two pretty young women entered a large uptown grocery one evening. . . .

"There's one thing I don't like about the clerks in this store," said one of them, while they waited for the salesman, "and that's the way they insist on telling you that you don't want what you do want and that you do want what you don't want. Every time I come in here I have the same experience, and I'm just tired of it. The next time it happens I'm going to tell the clerk just what I think of him."

At that moment a clerk approached and asked the young women what they wanted. The one who had so much to complain about pointed at one of a row of cracker tins and said: "I want a pound of those."

"Oh, no, you don't," said the clerk, suavely, "you want some of these, or these here; they're all very nice."

The young woman threw a glance which said: "What did I tell you?" at her companion, and turning to the clerk, said fiercely: "No, I don't, anything of the kind. I want these and no others."

"I beg your pardon," he began, "I thought—"

"Never mind what you thought," said the young woman. "I guess I know what I want. Now, just let me have a pound of those, please," and she turned to her companion with a look of triumph on her face, which plainly meant: "Didn't I squelch him?"

"Very well, madam," said the clerk, humbly, "but may I ask whether they are for yourself?"

"Well, of all the impertinent questions—" began the young woman, when her companion interrupted, and, turning to the clerk, said: "Why do you ask?"

"Oh, because they're dog biscuit[s]."[1]

Whether this 1896 story, reprinted in the *River Falls Journal*, was based on factual events or dreamed up for entertainment, it portrays a scene that may seem foreign to the contemporary shopper yet was very common to our ancestors. Today, we go to the store, fill a basket or cart, and check out. Many stores now offer a self-checkout option, eliminating the need for any direct contact between store personnel and customers. Today's independent method of shopping for groceries is so common that it is hard to imagine it ever being done differently. Historically, however, Americans who frequented grocers had a very different experience.

During a typical turn-of-the-century shopping trip, a grocery clerk behind a counter would welcome a shopper entering the establishment, take their order, and then gather the needed items. Technological advances eventually allowed customers to place grocery orders over the phone and have the goods delivered directly to their homes, a practice that became popular once again during the early months of the COVID-19 pandemic in 2020. Usually, customers would not pay for their order at the store but instead receive periodic bills.

The contemporary self-service grocery store concept was introduced by the Piggly Wiggly chain in Memphis, Tennessee, in 1916.[2] In Wisconsin, similar stores could be found as early as 1918, the year a Mineral Point grocer remodeled his entire store to launch the Groceteria, where customers could do their own shopping.[3] This reinvented grocery store proved to be a success in Mineral Point, growing in popularity because it was able to offer better prices. The new concept cut down on labor, a change that shoppers particularly welcomed during World War I.[4] Clerks could now spend their time shelving rather than filling individual orders. The store achieved further savings by eliminating the wasteful packaging needed for deliveries, and customers were spared the accompanying service fees.[5]

Despite the Groceteria's popularity in Mineral Point, the revolution of the grocery store in other parts of the state was a slow process. In 1920, the *Baraboo Weekly News*

## The GROCETERIA
### WILL BE OPEN FOR BUSINESS
## SATURDAY, OCTOBER 19

**Five patriotic reasons for the groceteria store:**

1. Eliminates telephone buying, which has been disapproved by the food administration.

2. Gives customers the benefit of the saving by eliminating delivery costs.

3. Gives customers the benefit of savings made by eliminating charge accounts.

4. Eliminates the element of waste in the process of deliveries, some of the most flagrant faults of the old system of retailing groceries.

5. Helps the labor situation by releasing for more essential work, ;he grocer's clerks.

IT IS PATRIOTIC TO CARRY A BASKET IN WAR TIMES.

### GROCETERIA
Successors to James Brewer Co.

**The Groceteria, a self-service grocery store in Mineral Point, opened in October of 1918.** *Iowa County Democrat,* October 17, 1918

reported a series of robberies of Piggly Wiggly stores in Chicago "where customers are permitted to gather packages of groceries from the shelves and pay at the exit, no clerks being employed."[6] As revealed by this concern that the self-service concept was an invitation for thieves, some Wisconsinites doubted that this type of store could stand the test of time. They likely wished to maintain the system that allowed them to order exactly thirty almonds for their almond casserole and watch as the clerks carefully counted them. Alas, over a century later, we either count our own almonds in the bulk food section or grab a pre-packaged bag off the shelf.

# Almond Casserole

*Nord Stern*, April 6, 1900[7]

Makes 6 servings

> 4 ounces butter
>
> 1 cup milk
>
> ¼ pound flour
>
> 2 ounces sugar
>
> 2 eggs, separated
>
> 30 almonds, chopped
>
> Fruit sauce, if desired (Note: Filling from the Rhubarb Tartlets recipe on page 158 works well.)

Mandelauflauf (sehr fein). Zwei Unzen Butter läßt man in einer Kasserolle zergehen, rührt ein viertel Pfund feines Mehl hinein, gießt nach und nach ein halbes Pint Milch zu und kocht einige Minuten auf gelindem Feuer einen zarten Teig, nimmt ihn vom Feuer, rührt zwei Eigelb, zwei Unzen Zucker, 30 Stück gehackte Mandeln, von zwei Eiweiß Schnee darunter und stellt es in einer gut bestrichenen Blechform eine viertel Stunde in den Ofen. Er geht hoch auf und sieht wie abgeriebener Napfkuchen aus; passend dazu ist Fruchtsauce. Diese Speise reicht für drei Personen; sind mehr Personen vorhanden, so nehme man von Allem genau das Doppelte.

Preheat oven to 350°F. Melt butter in a pot over low to medium heat. Once butter is melted, add milk and flour, and stir over low heat until it forms into a soft dough.

Take the pot off the stove and stir sugar, egg yolks, and almonds into the dough. Whip egg whites until they form firm peaks and carefully fold into the dough.

Transfer the dough to a small, buttered cake pan and bake for 15 to 30 minutes, depending on the thickness of the dough. To make sure the inside of the casserole is fully cooked, insert a toothpick. If it comes out clean, the casserole is done. Enjoy with fruit sauce.

# BEVERAGES

# 44
# CUPS OF ALL KINDS
## Specialized Drinkware

To anyone entertaining the popular belief that life back in the day was much simpler, historical drinkware begs to differ. While the shape and size of a drinking vessel may matter little to those simply seeking to quench their thirst, these elements seem to have been almost as important as the drink itself at formal occasions around the turn of the century—especially when it came to hot beverages. While the mug has become a hero of versatility in modern times, a diverse array of teacups, coffee cups, and chocolate cups once filled historical cabinets, and each specimen was perfectly customized to its intended use.

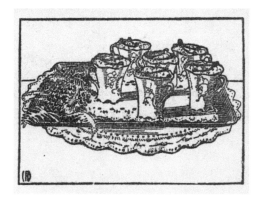

In this 1906 image, chocolate cups were used to serve a "New Year custard" garnished with wishbones cut from citron. *Telegraph-Courier,* January 18, 1906

Teacups were typically made of thin porcelain, with a wide mouth that tapered to a small base for sitting on a saucer. With a large surface area exposed to the air, hot tea could quickly cool to drinking temperature, and a teacup's dainty handle kept fingers just far enough from the liquid to avoid burned skin. Some tea drinkers were even known to pour a small amount of their beverage into the saucer, where it cooled down even faster before they slurped it off the dish. This practice, however, had fallen out of fashion by the late nineteenth century.[1]

In this time period, coffee was not brewed at the same high temperature as tea. Therefore, coffee cups were made of a thicker porcelain and had smaller openings, which helped retain the heat. Cups designed for the enjoyment of hot chocolate accounted for not just heat retention but also the beverage's consistency. A thick, frothy top layer of hot chocolate was considered by many to be the epitome of indulgence, but this layer could easily dissolve in a wide-mouthed cup. Hence, chocolate cups were very narrow—so narrow, in fact, that tall cups could be rather wobbly unless held up by a stabilizing saucer, and short ones looked like children's drinkware.

While it may seem excessive to have three different cups for tea, coffee, and hot chocolate, this was by no means an upper-class extravagance in the early 1900s. In 1914, Schuette Bros. Co. advertised a special sale of all three varieties made of "German, Japanese and French China in beautiful designs and colorings."[2] By then, elaborate patterns and ostentatious geometrical designs had also become affordable and popular in glassware commonly used for cold beverages.

**This "Pres Cut" glass punch bowl with cups was advertised as part of a giveaway in 1907.**
*Eagle River Review*, February 8, 1907

Drinking glasses had been in use for centuries, but glass manufacturing was revolutionized in the nineteenth century. In the 1820s, a newly invented American machine that pressed glass into steel molds allowed for the mass production of drinkware. By 1840, advances in the molds enabled glassmakers to produce pressed-glass goblets with designs similar to those featured on much more expensive cut-glass varieties. This opened up the ornate glassware market to a larger consumer base. During the next two decades, the development of cheaper glass materials made glassware even more affordable, further democratizing fancy punch bowls, goblets, and tall cups to hold refreshing lemonade—and turning glassware with intricate patterns into everyday household items.[3]

# Fruit Lemonade

*Odanah Star,* August 16, 1912[4]

Makes 12 cups

2 cups raspberries

4 cups sugar

4 cups chopped pineapple

2 cups orange juice

1 cup lemon juice

Mash raspberries with a fork or wooden spoon and strain them to collect about 1 cup of raspberry juice.

In a pot combine 2 quarts of cold water, sugar, and chopped pineapple. Boil for 20 minutes.

Add orange juice, lemon juice, and raspberry juice. Cool, strain, and dilute to taste with ice water.

## FRUIT LEMONADE.

The following recipe should be sufficient to serve a dozen persons: Boil together two quarts of cold water, four cupfuls of sugar and four cupfuls of chopped pineapple for twenty minutes. Add to this two cupfuls of orange juice, one cupful of lemon juice and one cupful of raspberry juice. Cool, strain and dilute with ice water.

Another recipe calls for one cupful of sugar, one cupful of hot tea infusion, three-fourths of a cupful of orange juice, a few slices of orange, one-third of a cupful of lemon juice, one pint of ginger ale, one pint of lithia water and some maraschino cherries. Pour the tea over the sugar and as soon as the sugar is dissolved add the fruit juices. Strain into punch bowl over a large piece of ice and just before serving add ginger ale, lithia, slices of orange and cherries.

Pouring boiling water over lemons is said to double the amount of juice they will yield.

# 45

## DOCTOR'S ORDERS

### Alcohol Consumption during Prohibition

In the years before the nationwide prohibition of alcohol, recipes for alcoholic beverages in Wisconsin newspapers were numerous. Even local ice was used in mixed drinks, as the *Manitowoc Tribune* noted in 1876: "And now Saint Louis cock-tails are to be toned down with ice from the Manitowoc river. Within the past week one hundred car-loads have been sent from here direct."[1]

In fact, recipes for apple toddies, shrubs, and brandy smashes appeared next to early articles promoting the temperance movement. In 1897, the *Wood County Reporter* published a recipe for a blackberry cordial that included fresh berries, cloves, allspice, cinnamon, sugar, and, of course, brandy.[2] An 1896 *Watertown Republican* article about "cooling drinks" offered a recipe for the mint julep.[3] And an interesting creation called the "Mince Pie Cocktail" appeared in the *Vilas County News* that same year. The drink called for "Jersey applejack, yellow chartreuse bitters and a dash of the oil of lemon rind."[4] As Americans' enthusiasm for mixed drinks grew near the end of the nineteenth century, the temperance movement also gained steam, and by 1920, the liquors used to mix those drinks were banned.

**U. S. LED MOVE FOR TEMPERANCE**

Many Societies to Fight Alcohol Organized Early in Nation's History.

**WOMEN ACTIVE AS LEADERS**

**An article on the history of the temperance movement was printed in the *Washburn Times* in 1919.** *Washburn Times, February 6, 1919*

Despite the aims of the temperance movement, Prohibition did not entirely stop the flow of alcohol in Wisconsin. A common loophole was provided by physicians, who were permitted to prescribe alcohol for "medicinal purposes," as the *Wausau Pilot* reported in 1922: "Unadulterated whiskey and colored alcohol is being sold as liquor of medicinal benefit to hundreds of sick persons in Wisconsin, according to statements by federal prohibition enforcement officers."[5] Permits to prescribe alcohol cost applicants ten dollars (roughly one hundred fifty dollars today) and they were in high demand; more than a thousand permits were applied for in the state in 1925 alone.[6]

A patient who was prescribed alcohol for medicinal purposes could have a prescription written for a variety of intoxicating substances, including wine, distilled spirits, and other vaguely titled "alcoholic medicinal preparations," though each patient was allowed no more than six quarts per year.[7] Though perhaps some people could claim their alcohol was truly for medicinal use, most patients visiting their physicians for this prescription knew it was an easy way to come home with a pint of booze for five or six dollars.[8] Some Wisconsinites launched a valiant, if slightly comical, movement to get beer on the list of alcoholic substances that could be prescribed for medicinal purposes. The Kenosha *Telegraph-Courier* reported in 1921, "It will not be a hard proposition for any Kenoshan who has not lost the taste for real beer, to quench his thirst at some of the Kenosha drug stores if the recent ruling made by the secretary of the treasury goes into effect."[9]

While alcohol consumption moved into pharmacies and speakeasies for the thirteen years that Prohibition was in effect, newspaper recipes also adjusted to the new law of the land. Recipes for nonalcoholic versions of popular cocktails appeared. Milk punch, for example, a drink historically made with brandy, was featured in a recipe that called for just milk, sugar, eggs, nutmeg, and shaved ice.[10] However, in some households this family-friendly concoction was probably accompanied by a little splash of something extra prescribed by a local physician.

# Milk Punch

*Wausau Pilot*, August 10, 1922[11]

Makes 2 servings

1 egg

1 teaspoon sugar

7 ounces milk

6 ounces shaved ice

Grated nutmeg

MILK PUNCH — For each person beat thoroughly an egg with a teaspoon of sugar; add to this two-thirds of a goblet of shaved ice and milk; cover closely with a shaker or a large goblet inverted and shake up and down until the ice is nearly melted. Dust the top with grated nutmeg.

In a glass, beat egg and sugar thoroughly. Add milk and shaved ice. Cover with a shaker and shake up and down until the ice is nearly melted. Dust the top with grated nutmeg.

## 46

# SWISS MISS HOT COCOA

## A Wisconsin Original

In 1950, the United States entered the Korean War, and a Menomonie dairy began supplying American troops with powdered coffee creamer. To meet the strict terms of the military contract, the Sanna Dairy Engineers company produced so much that they were left with a surplus of individual packets of creamer at the end of the war. At that time, the powder was still perishable due to the butterfat left in the product.[1] Not wanting to waste the overstock, the mechanical engineer Charles Sanna, whose father had founded the company, started experimenting with using the powdered creamer in family recipes for hot chocolate. Sanna enlisted his children as taste testers. With their help, he developed a product that would have a long-lasting impact on how we prepare hot chocolate to this day.[2]

The tradition of drinking hot chocolate has been around for millennia and originated in Mesoamerica, the home of the cacao tree (see "Eating Chocolate" on page 149). The seeds, or cacao beans, were harvested, fermented, dried, and crushed into a powder. The powder was then mixed with water and spices to create a savory drink.[3] Over time, as the cacao bean made its way around the globe, as different sweeteners became more widely available, and as milk

**COCOA AND CHOCOLATE**

———

TWO READILY DIGESTED, HIGHLY
NOURISHING BEVERAGES.

———

Have Real Food Value and Should
Take the Place of Tea or Coffee
for Children — Few With
Whom They Disagree.

———

This 1913 article praised chocolate for its nutritional properties. *Wausau Pilot*, May 13, 1913

was introduced to the beverage, the taste and preparation of hot chocolate evolved and its popularity grew worldwide. By 1913, the *Wausau Pilot* praised hot chocolate for its nutritional benefits, calling it "a highly nutritious as well as palatable drink, far superior to either tea or coffee."[4]

With his powder product, Sanna built on an ancient culinary tradition to solve his overstock issue and, at the same time, meet the modern desire for convenience. His invention was the beginning of instant hot chocolate—a product that allowed Americans to prepare a delicious and rich chocolatey drink with the addition of just hot water or milk. "Brown Swiss," as it was initially named, was first marketed toward airlines and restaurants, but the packets were so well-liked that they regularly disappeared into customers' and employees' pockets. Sanna continued to experiment, eventually creating a cheaper, shelf-stable product that could be sold directly to consumers at their local grocery stores.[5] Swiss Miss finally hit the shelves in 1961. While using instant hot chocolate in a time crunch is convenient and can be seen as a celebration of Wisconsin history, we highly recommend that you take the time, once in a while, to prepare a more old-fashioned chocolaty concoction and sip it slowly from a nice cup.

# Hot Chocolate

*Wauwatosa News,* December 14, 1917[6]

Makes 4 servings

### Hot chocolate

1 ½ ounces unsweetened chocolate

¼ cup sugar

1 pinch salt

3 cups milk

### Whipped cream

1 cup heavy whipping cream

1 tablespoon sugar

> **Hot Chocolate.**—One and one-half squares of unsweetened chocolate, one-quarter cupful sugar, few grains salt, a cupful boiling water three cupfuls milk. Scald milk, melt chocolate (in small saucepan placed over hot water), add sugar, salt and, gradually, boiling water. When smooth place on range and boil one minute. Add to scalded milk, mill and serve in chocolate cups with whipped cream. To mill chocolate beat until froth forms on top, preventing scum. Use Dover egg beater.

For hot chocolate: bring 1 cup water to boil. At the same time, melt chocolate in a water bath or a double boiler. Add sugar and salt to the molten chocolate and slowly stir in the boiling water. Take the pot containing this mixture out of the water bath and place it directly on the stove to boil for at least 1 minute.

In a separate pot, bring milk to a simmer. Stir simmering milk into the chocolate mixture.

For whipped cream: Whip cream and sugar with a whisk, Dover eggbeater, or trusty kitchen mixer until firm peaks form.

Serve hot chocolate in a fancy chocolate cup topped with whipped cream, and enjoy.

# TEA TIME

## The Ceylon Tea Campaign

European colonizers had been enjoying tea for quite some time before they set foot in the area that would come to be known as Wisconsin. Europeans first came in contact with the plant and beverage in East India in the sixteenth century. They began importing tea to their continent, where by the 1600s, it was enjoyed by members of all social classes. Hence, it is not surprising that European immigrants to the US also consumed the steeped hot beverage. Black and green teas, as well as flavored varieties, were readily available in nineteenth-century Wisconsin. An 1845 advertisement in the *Southport Telegraph*, for example, offered "fresh and fine flavored Green Tea" at three cents per pound at the local grocer.[1]

The difference between black and green tea is not that they derive from different plants but that black tea is fermented and green tea is steamed before it is dried.[2] Both varieties were consumed in the United States in the 1800s. And although the term *tea party* in the context of American history is not necessarily known as an enjoyable festivity, tea was served—both hot and cold—at social events during this time period. Iced tea was even thought to have health benefits, as the *Kenosha Telegraph* stated: "High medical authority recommends iced tea as a summer drink. For relief of thirst and cooling the blood when heated it is claimed to be the best drink that can be taken."[3]

A new kind of tea became available in the late nineteenth century. While people in the United States were used to purchasing simply "tea," which was usually imported from Japan or China, now they saw "Ceylon tea" appear in their dry goods stores. Ceylon tea originates from Sri Lanka, which, until 1972, was known to the Western

**Three friends share tea outdoors, ca. 1890.**
WHI IMAGE ID 11629

world as Ceylon, a name given by the Portuguese who colonized the island. Local farmers in Sri Lanka had begun growing tea after the British first brought it to the country from China in 1824. The growing conditions for tea were ideal on the South Asian island, and plantation owners began to export some of the harvest. However, international sales did not pick up until after the Ceylon tea traders' association launched a large marketing campaign that branded the tea as Ceylon tea and, ultimately, increased the consumption of Sri Lankan tea in the United States by 100,000 percent.[4]

In Wisconsin newspapers, Ceylon tea appeared as early as the 1880s, but mentions became much more prevalent in the 1910s. Advertisements proclaimed the tea's superiority not just due to its flavor but also because of, as the *River Falls Journal* phrased it in 1910, the "modern Anglo-Saxon" processing standards that were applied during harvest and handling.[5] Rooted in racist stereotypes, these ads marketed the mostly British-produced Ceylon tea as a cleaner product than that grown in countries with long tea-growing traditions like China and Japan.

Readers may notice that this 1915 recipe for a Hongkong Cooler calls for iced Ceylon tea. This name makes no sense, geographically speaking, since Hong Kong is located nearly 2,500 miles northeast of Sri Lanka. However, the recipe is an indication of how much more popular Ceylon tea was at the time and how accessible it was for Wisconsinites.

# Hongkong Cooler

*Iron County News*, May 1, 1915[6]

Makes 2 servings

3 tablespoons Ceylon tea (black)

4 tablespoons sugar

3 lemon slices

2 cloves

4 maraschino cherries

Shaved ice

3 ounces rum

2 sprigs mint

1 tablespoon powdered sugar

Candied orange peel (see Candied
   Orange Peel recipe on page 185),
   if desired

6 tablespoons crushed pineapple,
   if desired

**Hongkong Cooler**—Pour one quart of boiling water over three tablespoonfuls of Ceylon tea. Let steep four or five minutes, strain and cool, adding four tablespoonfuls of sugar, three slices of lemon, two cloves and four maraschino cherries.

When ready to serve, pour into tall glasses half full of shaved ice and add a dash of Jamaica rum to each glass, placing a spray of mint that has been dipped first into iced water, then into powdered sugar. A strip of candied orange peel may be added and three tablespoonfuls of pineapple, if one wants to make the punch more elaborate and complicated in appearance.

Steep tea in 1 quart boiling water for 4 to 5 minutes. Strain the tea and add sugar, lemon slices, cloves, and maraschino cherries. Let cool. When ready to serve, pour into tall glasses half full of shaved ice. Add a dash of rum to each glass. Dust mint with powdered sugar and use as garnish.

A strip of candied orange peel and crushed pineapple may be added, if desired, to make the punch more elaborate in appearance.

# PICKLES AND PRESERVES

# 48

# KEEPING COOL WITH SUMMER KITCHENS

## The Heat of Historical Cookstoves

The concept of cooking exclusively inside our homes, regardless of the season or the weather, is a relatively new one, brought on largely by advances in home technology. Before the invention of modern cookstoves that use heat-efficient technology, households in Wisconsin and across the country had to adapt their homes to deal with the heat emanating from their wood- and coal-burning stoves.

During Wisconsin winters, these stoves did not create much discomfort; instead, they provided homes with a built-in heating source. In the state's occasionally sweltering and often humid summers, however, the prospect of cooking over a wood-burning stove was unappealing at best. To mitigate this problem, some Wisconsinites added summer kitchens to their homes. "Henry Bronson has erected a new building back of his residence to be used as a summer kitchen," the *Wood County Reporter* announced in 1886.[1] Freestanding and often located behind the main house, this building housed the cookstove and other kitchen implements, as the *Kenosha Telegraph* described in 1876: "Several

**House and Lot For Sale.**

One of the pleasantest residences in the city, situated in a good locality, surrounded by fine grounds, is offered for sale at a bargain. House contains six rooms with a summer kitchen, closets, cellar, etc. Possession will be given in a few weeks. For further particulars apply to or address

S. MITCHELL,

4w3   P. O. Address: Lancaster, Wis.

**A Lancaster real estate listing from 1883 highlights the property's summer kitchen.**
*Grant County Herald,* March 29, 1883

This 1907 Standard Oil Company ad proposes an oil cook stove as a cooler alternative to other ranges. *Baraboo News*, May 29, 1907

residents have adopted the detached kitchen for summer use. This is a building for culinary purposes, separate from the main building; thus preventing the steam, smell and heat arising from it pervading the house. During the sultry portion of the summer, this arrangement is a pleasant one."[2]

Summer kitchens grew increasingly common throughout the nineteenth century. Many residents considered the comfort and convenience they provided to be worth the cost and effort of building an additional structure on their property. In real estate listings in Wisconsin newspapers, summer kitchens were commonly mentioned as desirable features of properties for sale.

While offering comfort, a summer kitchen could also act as a safety feature. At the time, house fires often started in the kitchen, but if a fire started in a summer kitchen, the primary residence could be left unscathed. In 1903, for example, an article in the *Wisconsin Tobacco Reporter* of Edgerton related: "The fire alarm awoke the village at 5 o'clock Sunday morning. It proved to be the summer kitchen and tool house on the Shuman farm near town. The kitchen was some distance from the house and the wind being favorable saved the dwelling."[3]

As the twentieth century ushered new technologies into Wisconsin households, the summer kitchen started to become a relic of the past. Gas, oil, and the new electric cookstoves could accomplish all that wood- and coal-burning stoves were able to without generating the same enormous heat output (see "Wired with Excitement" on page 100). Advertisements emphasized the stoves' efficiency and appealed directly to home cooks. One in the *Baraboo News* advised, "Don't swelter this summer with the temperature at 110. Get a New Perfection Wick Blue Flame Oil Stove and have a cool kitchen." Another in the *Wisconsin Tobacco Reporter* of Edgerton warned, "With summer days come those hot, hot kitchens. . . . Then too, think how easy, clean and convenient it is to cook by electricity."[4] Separate buildings were no longer necessary to house these newfangled stoves in the warmer months, and house plans featured in Wisconsin's newspapers in the early decades of the twentieth century incorporated the kitchen in, not outside, the house.[5]

Though they are far removed from the needs of our contemporary lives, summer kitchens were once an integral feature of houses across the state. The original readers who prepared this recipe for pickled peaches in 1903 may have conducted the process in their summer kitchens, finding refuge afterward in a cool main house untouched by cooking heat.

# Sweet Pickled Peaches

*Wauwatosa News,* October 31, 1903[6]

Makes 4 to 5 quart-size canning jars

20 medium peaches

4 pounds brown sugar

1 quart apple cider vinegar

2 ounces cinnamon sticks, broken
   into pieces

40–60 cloves

**Sweet Pickled Peaches.**

Prepare a syrup of four pounds of brown sugar, one quart of best cider vinegar, and two ounces of stick cinnamon broken in pieces. Boil all together twenty minutes. Have peaches ready, having previously dipped them quickly into boiling water and rubbed off fur with a crash towel. Stick two or three cloves into each peach—not more for the clove darkens the peach. Put half of peaches into syrup at a time, and cook until clear and tender. Drain out and put into jars, and pour boiling syrup over them, filling jar full. Seal.

Quickly dip peaches into boiling water with a slotted spoon, transfer them to an ice water bath, and use a dish towel to rub off the furry skin.

In a pot, mix brown sugar, apple cider vinegar, and broken cinnamon sticks. Boil the mixture for 20 minutes to make a syrup.

Stick 2 to 3 cloves into each peach and cook them in the syrup in batches until clear and tender.

Place peaches into jars and pour the hot syrup over them. Use your preferred canning method to seal the jars. For short-term storage, keep in the fridge after they cool.

Note: We recommend serving on a rainy fall day with vanilla ice cream.

# THE AGE OF APRONS

## Protective Kitchen Garments

Pickling walnuts is no easy feat. The process is quite messy, and anyone attempting it would be wise to wear gloves and an apron to protect their hands and clothing from the permanent stains of walnut husks. While aprons are still a relatively common household garment, some modern home cooks might think of them as nostalgic items worn by their grandmothers. Advances in the technology of washing machines and the industrialization of clothing production have rendered the apron less of a necessity in today's kitchens. Before the invention of the washing machine, doing laundry was a laborious and time-intensive process involving washboards, elbow grease, and clotheslines. Even the early washing machines of the 1800s required the continuous rotation of a handle or crank of a wheel, by hand, to operate.

If an item of clothing is permanently ruined today, a replacement can easily be bought at the store. Before the 1900s, clothing was often homemade, and a typical wardrobe contained only a few items for different seasons and occasions during the year. Ready-to-wear clothing was expensive; it was made with high quality materials and without modern manufacturing techniques, which have since cheapened labor costs and end products. For example, a common silk blouse in 1899 was advertised in Edgerton's *Wisconsin Tobacco Reporter* for $3.49, which is roughly $123 today.[1] This helps explain why the apron was a steady companion to home cooks before the twentieth century.

Many newspapers published apron designs that readers could sew at home. Functional aprons that covered much of the body were popular for doing kitchen work, and daintier aprons with ruffles or bows were advertised as being ideal for hosts serving guests in their homes. The most popular apron materials were cotton and linen, given their durable nature and fact that they could be easily washed. The *Washburn Times* emphasized in 1914 that the apron must "be made to stand weekly tubbing at least, and substantial materials are the only kind worth making up."[2] Showier aprons could be made out of silk and would often cover less of a hostess's body to better display her dress underneath. Needlework was often incorporated into these types of aprons, adding cheerful floral or geometric patterns. As a 1910 article in the *Watertown Leader* stated:

This working apron made of blue and white percale is pictured with a sleeve protector.
*Vilas County News*, September 18, 1912

> The apron above all else must be the last word in fineness and exquisite daintiness—even though very simple materials must be fine. Hand embroidered aprons are the prettiest model in the whole apron family, and any girl or woman who knows how to embroider should lose no time in adding one or two of these attractive trifles to her summer outfit, or make one or two for the coming winter.[3]

In addition to apron patterns, newspapers advertised sewing patterns for sleeve covers, as illustrated in the 1912 *Vilas County News*.[4] Sleeve covers were meant to protect clothing from spills and splashes on the forearms, an area neglected by other traditional protective kitchen garments. Unlike the apron, sleeve covers have since fallen out of favor. Considering their practicality, especially when dealing with hot grease, however, it might be a good idea to dig up those historical sewing patterns and initiate their modern-day comeback.

# Pickled Walnuts

*Dodgeville Chronicle*, June 18, 1875[5]

Makes 100 pickled walnuts

100 walnuts (green and unripe, picked
directly from the tree)

3–4 pounds salt, divided

½ gallon white vinegar

2 ounces black pepper

3 ounces ginger, bruised

¾ teaspoon mace

¼–½ ounce cloves

4 ounces mustard seed

—To pickle walnuts gather them while a pin can pierce them easily, for when once the shell can be felt they have ceased to be in a proper state for it. Make sufficient brine to cover them well, with six ounces of salt to the gallon of water; take off the scum which will rise to the surface as the salt dissolves, throw in the walnuts and stir them night and morning; change the brine every three days, and if they are wanted for immediate eating leave them in it for twelve days; if not drain them from it in nine, spread them on dishes and let them remain exposed to the air until they become black; this will be in twelve hours. Make a pickle for them with something more than half a gallon of vinegar to the hundred, a teaspoonful of salt, two ounces of black pepper, three of bruised ginger, a dram of mace and from a quarter to half an ounce of cloves, and four ounces of mustard seed. Boil the whole of these together for about five minutes, have the walnuts ready in a stone jar, and pour it on them as it is taken from the fire. When the pickle is quite cold cover the jar securely and store it in a dry place. Keep the walnuts well covered with vinegar, and boil that which is added to them.—*N. Y. News.*

Gather walnuts in the early summer while they are still green and a pin can pierce them easily. Once the hard shell has formed on the inside, they have ceased to be in a proper state for pickling. Note: When handling the walnuts, wear rubber gloves and use kitchenware that can be stained.

Using a fork, prick the husk of each walnut multiple times. Make enough salt water to cover them well, using 6 ounces of salt to every 1 gallon of water. Throw in walnuts and stir them night and morning for 9 to 12 days. Change the salt water every 3 days. If the walnuts are wanted for immediate eating, leave them in for 12 days; if not, drain them after 9 days, spread them on baking sheets, and let them remain exposed to the air until they become black, approximately 12 hours.

In a pot, make a pickling brine using ½ gallon of vinegar, 1 teaspoon salt, and the pepper, ginger, mace, cloves, and mustard seed. Boil the mixture for about five minutes.

Place walnuts into sterile canning jars and pour the boiling brine over them. Place the cooled jars into the fridge or use preferred canning method to prepare for long-term storage.

# (50)
# PRESERVING APPLES
## A Consideration of Alcohol and Friendship

Apple trees are not native to North America; therefore, every apple tree we see here today is, in one way or another, a product of planting efforts. In some historic Wisconsin newspapers, like the *Southport Telegraph* in 1840, staff tried to persuade readers to plant fruit trees: "Were every farmer and other person, who is possessed of a sufficient spot of ground, to devote a little time and expense to the planting of fruit trees, Wisconsin in a few years would abound in fruit as rich and delicious as in any other country."[1] Many listened, began to plant, and ended up with bushels of fruit at the end of the harvest season. As a result, an abundance of apple recipes can be found in newspapers from around the state, suggesting a plethora of ways that a plentiful harvest could be processed. While the papers teemed with recipes for pies, pastries, other desserts, and the occasional fresh apple snack, readers were also clearly hungry for ways to preserve the nutritious fruit long term in the days before modern refrigeration at home and in food transport.

A popular option for enjoying apples long past picking time was to turn them into cider. Before Prohibition, virtually all cider was alcoholic. After apples were pressed, the resulting fresh cider was kept at seventy degrees Fahrenheit for sixteen to twenty days to ferment. During this process, the yeast bacteria turned the sugar of the pressed apples into alcohol. Once the preferred alcohol content and level of sweetness was reached, the cider was cooled down to stop the fermentation process; then it was stored to be enjoyed at a later date by the whole family.[2] While proponents of the temperance movement warned against cider consumption, especially by children, the

*Northern Wisconsin Advertiser* proclaimed in 1904: "Cider is considered by physicians to be a specially wholesome drink, and is recommended as an antidote to excessive meat-eating and for rheumatism, gout and all other diseases due to a uric acid diathesis."[3] While nowadays we would not recommend hard cider consumption for health reasons nor for the entire family, we do recommend the more family-friendly apple-preserving alternative of apple butter.

To make apple butter, Victorian folks combined apples with spices and sugar, then cooked the ingredients down into a delicious spread, which could be stored for much longer than a fresh apple. Many recipes call for the fruit to be cooked in cider, probably to prevent it from burning in the kettle, which typically hung directly over an open flame. It is less clear whether such recipes intended for the cider to be fresh and unfermented or alcoholic. After sampling the results of an 1881 recipe made with both fresh and hard cider, twenty-first-century blind taste testers actually

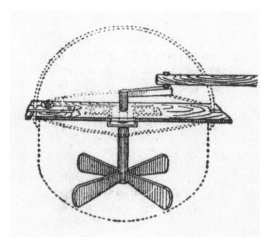

This DIY apple butter stirrer was intended to fit inside a kettle, represented by the dotted lines on this image. *Watertown Leader*, October 27, 1911

preferred the sweeter fresh cider apple butter. Even when made with the alcoholic cider, though, the finished product likely does not contain any alcohol—according to modern science, that is. For many years, people assumed that alcohol simply evaporated when cooked. It wasn't until the early 1990s that scientists experimented with different recipes to study alcohol retention in food and concluded that alcohol evaporation depends on cooking temperature, time, and the surface area of the cooking vessel.[4] Since apple butter was historically cooked in a large kettle and boiled over a direct flame for many hours, it is likely that the resulting product would not have retained any alcohol.

One challenging aspect of making apple butter was its cooking time: around fourteen hours. The recipe included here suggests that anyone attempting it should rope their friends into joining them for the long day of apple butter–making: "Apple butter is a tedious thing to make. It is best to have a merry making over the apple-paring and stirring, as it is very heavy work for one or two persons."[5] The recipe also includes the helpful suggestion to use "an oaken stave pierced with holes and fastened to a long handle—a broomstick" in order to stir the mixture at a safe distance from the fire.[6] Even with modern stoves and cookware, which severely cut down the cooking time, the process of making apple butter remains a great opportunity for friends to gather and take turns stirring. Our advice, though, is to choose those friends wisely. No one wants to end up like the poor young fellow in the 1870s whose friends got too tired and abandoned him at the fire to finish the spread by himself.[7] The first time we made this apple butter, we did so together and enjoyed not just the smell of the cooking apples and spices but also the time we shared around the stove. This recipe encouraged us to slow down and engage in conversation while we took turns stirring. In the end, we were rewarded with a taste of history, as well as friendship.

# Apple Butter with Cider

*Watertown Republican,* December 14, 1881[8]

Makes about 4 cups

2 quarts apples (about 8 to 12 apples)

2 quarts fresh apple cider

2 cups sugar

1 ½ teaspoons ground cinnamon

1 ½ teaspoons ground cloves

Core, peel, and chop apples and add to a large pot with cider. Bring to a simmer and stir often to prevent the mixture from burning. Add water a little at a time as needed to prevent burning. After the apple pieces have cooked down into apple sauce, add sugar and spices. Continue to cook and stir until the mixture is so stiff that a spoon will stand up in it. This may take a few hours.

Fill jars with apple butter. Enjoy on a slice of bread immediately or store in the refrigerator for several weeks. For long-term storage, use preferred canning method.

### APPLE BUTTER.

Boil four gallons of cider for three hours, skimming it. Have the apples pared and cored, and put them in gradually; as they boil down fill up with more apples. Have an oaken stave pierced with holes and fastened to a long handle—a broomstick is the best—so that you can stand at a distance from the kettle. It must be stirred continually to prevent its burning. If you have your cider on to boil by 10 in the morning, the apple butter ought to be all cooked by 12 at night. Sweeten it to taste with light, brown sugar, but the sugar must not be added until about an hour before it comes off the fire, as it burns more easily after the sugar is in. Add cinnamon and cloves to taste when you put the sugar in. When it is done it must be so stiff that a spoon will stand up in it. Apple butter is a tedious thing to make. It is best to have a merry-making over the apple-paring and stirring, as it is very heavy work for one or two persons. A gay party in a country house undertook it a few seasons ago, but long before midnight all had given out, leaving one strong-armed young fellow alone to finish it. Apple butter must be cooked in a very large kettle, a perfectly new tin boiler, or a copper kettle. There is no use in making up a small quantity, as it takes just as much time as to cook a barrel of cider. If made according to this receipt, it is sure to keep.

# ACKNOWLEDGMENTS

When it comes to this book, there is no such thing as too many cooks in the kitchen. This book would not have been possible without the many people who have supported us along the way. Kaleb, Madita, and Paden, who had front row seats to witness the craziness that unfolded in our kitchens, were always willing to taste test, share their opinions, and help us carve out time to experiment and write. John, Maureen, and Eli consistently volunteered their taste buds, were eager to listen to our new discoveries, and never shied away from getting in harm's way. Halley, arguably one of our biggest advocators, helped us believe that this little hobby of ours would be worth sharing. Our families, who may not always understand what we do, continue to support us, nevertheless.

In the process of turning our manuscript into a book, we feel enormously fortunate to have met Liz, our wonderful editor, who immediately understood our vision and helped us enhance it.

Food photography is not easy, and the dishes in this book would have looked a lot different if John and Andrew had not shared their knowledge and generously lent us equipment to make our food shine bright even during dark winter afternoons. Many of the vintage and artisanal plates, bowls, and glasses featured in our photographs were generously provided by Megan and Lauren.

We are grateful for our colleagues at the Wisconsin Historical Society and their passion for history. The expertise they have shared with us over the years is priceless and has shaped our approach to working with historical recipes and cooking techniques.

Lastly, projects like this book depend hugely on the collection and preservation of historical material. The folks working for the National Digital Newspaper Program, the Library of Congress, the National Endowment for the Humanities, and the Wisconsin Historical Society work tirelessly to make historic newspapers, such as the ones we referenced in this book, accessible to all.

# NOTES

## Breakfast Parties

1. "News of the Week," *Washburn Times*, April 13, 1911, https://chroniclingamerica.loc.gov/lccn/sn85040437/1911-04-13/ed-1/seq-5/.

2. *Wisconsin Tobacco Reporter* (Edgerton), July 23, 1915, https://chroniclingamerica.loc.gov/lccn/sn86086586/1915-07-23/ed-1/seq-2/; "Local Happenings," *Wisconsin Tobacco Reporter* (Edgerton), April 15, 1910, https://chroniclingamerica.loc.gov/lccn/sn86086586/1910-04-15/ed-1/seq-5/; "Breakfast Party," *Wisconsin Weekly Blade* (Madison), August 26, 1922, https://chroniclingamerica.loc.gov/lccn/sn84025842/1922-08-26/ed-1/seq-1/.

3. "The Park and Lake," *Iowa County Democrat*, August 24, 1922, https://chroniclingamerica.loc.gov/lccn/sn86086852/1922-08-24/ed-1/seq-1/.

4. "Society Items," *Wausau Pilot*, August 27, 1918, https://chroniclingamerica.loc.gov/lccn/sn85040749/1918-08-27/ed-1/seq-5/.

5. "Shirred Eggs," *Mineral Point Tribune*, February 10, 1887, https://chroniclingamerica.loc.gov/lccn/sn86086770/1887-02-10/ed-1/seq-6/.

6. *River Falls Journal*, February 28, 1895, https://chroniclingamerica.loc.gov/lccn/sn85033255/1895-02-28/ed-1/seq-3/.

7. "More Good Things to Eat," *Watertown Weekly Leader*, June 1, 1915, https://chroniclingamerica.loc.gov/lccn/sn85040721/1915-06-01/ed-1/seq-7/.

8. "Try These Fritters," *Vilas County News*, April 26, 1911, https://chroniclingamerica.loc.gov/lccn/sn85040613/1911-04-26/ed-1/seq-10/.

## À La Mode and Ouh Là Là

1. Biddy Bye, "Eggs a la Mode; That Is, French," *Wisconsin Weekly Blade* (Madison), June 12, 1919, https://chroniclingamerica.loc.gov/lccn/sn84025842/1919-06-12/ed-1/seq-5/.

2. "French Housekeeping," *Wisconsin Tobacco Reporter* (Edgerton), April 15, 1904, https://chroniclingamerica.loc.gov/lccn/sn86086586/1904-04-15/ed-1/seq-6.

3. "French Soup Made without Meat," *Dodgeville Chronicle*, February 17, 1871, https://chroniclingamerica.loc.gov/lccn/sn85033019/1871-02-17/ed-1/seq-2.

4. "Two Fancy Summer Dishes," *Grant County Herald*, October 6, 1909, https://chroniclingamerica.loc.gov/lccn/sn85033133/1909-10-06/ed-1/seq-6.

5. "Pretty Party Given by College Girls," *River Falls Journal*, December 27, 1906, https://chroniclingamerica.loc.gov/lccn/sn85033255/1906-12-27/ed-1/seq-6.

6. "Rancid Butter," *Southport Telegraph* (Kenosha), August 18, 1847, https://chroniclingamerica.loc.gov/lccn/sn85040303/1847-08-18/ed-1/seq-1.

7. "Hints to Housekeepers," *Watertown Republican*, February 11, 1891, https://chroniclingamerica.loc.gov/lccn/sn85033295/1891-02-11/ed-1/seq-6.

8. "How to Make a Bath Sachet," *Wood County Reporter*, February 22, 1906, https://chroniclingamerica.loc.gov/lccn/sn85033078/1906-02-22/ed-1/seq-3.

9. "Decay of French Cuisine," *Manitowoc Pilot,* November 18, 1897, https://chroniclingamerica.loc.gov/lccn/sn85033139/1897-11-18/ed-1/seq-1.

10. Bye, "Eggs A La Mode."

## Wisconsin's Aluminum Cookware

1. "Mirro Aluminum Company," Wisconsin Historical Society, n.d., www.wisconsinhistory.org/Records/Article/CS2509.

2. James M. Rock, "A Growth Industry: The Wisconsin Aluminum Cookware Industry 1893–1920," *Wisconsin Magazine of History* 55, no. 2 (Winter 1971–1972): 91.

3. Rock, "A Growth Industry," 96.

4. *Wauwatosa News*, June 16, 1922, https://chroniclingamerica.loc.gov/lccn/sn86086499/1922-06-16/ed-1/seq-8/; *River Falls Journal*, August 31, 1922, https://chroniclingamerica.loc.gov/lccn/sn85033255/1922-08-31/ed-1/seq-5/.

5. Rock, "A Growth Industry," 89.

6. "Alum. Goods Increases Capital," *Manitowoc Pilot*, June 24, 1920, https://chroniclingamerica.loc.gov/lccn/sn85033139/1920-06-24/ed-1/seq-1/.

7. "Breakfast Puffs," *Vernon County Censor*, October 28, 1914, https://chroniclingamerica.loc.gov/lccn/sn85040451/1914-10-28/ed-1/seq-3/.

## Wild Rice

1. Thomas Pecore Weso, *Good Seeds: A Menominee Indian Food Memoir* (Madison: Wisconsin Historical Society Press, 2016), 48.

2. "Wild Rice Good for Human Food," *Iowa County Democrat*, October 12, 1922, https://chroniclingamerica.loc.gov/lccn/sn86086852/1922-10-12/ed-1/seq-6/.

3. "News Items," *Prescott Journal*, January 18, 1868, https://chroniclingamerica.loc.gov/lccn/sn85033221/1868-01-18/ed-1/seq-1.

4. "Sees Wild Rice as Coming Food Crop in America," *Washburn Times*, April 8, 1920, https://chroniclingamerica.loc.gov/lccn/sn85040437/1920-04-08/ed-1/seq-6.

5. "Wild Rice," *Southport Telegraph* (Kenosha), November 2, 1841, https://chroniclingamerica.loc.gov/lccn/sn85040303/1841-11-02/ed-1/seq-3/.

6. "Wild Rice."

7. "Saturday," *Baraboo Weekly News*, October 11, 1917, https://chroniclingamerica.loc.gov/lccn/sn86086068/1917-10-11/ed-1/seq-10/; "Will Plant Wild Rice," *Iron County News*, October 21, 1922, https://chroniclingamerica.loc.gov/lccn/sn85040652/1922-10-21/ed-1/seq-1/.

8. "Hints from Scotland," *Iron County News*, March 14, 1914, https://chroniclingamerica.loc.gov/lccn/sn85040652/1914-03-14/ed-1/seq-6/.

## Eating in a Fresh-Air Fashion

1. "Make Down-River Trip Via Baraboo: Portage Young Men Start on Unique Camping Expedition," *Baraboo News*, August 17, 1911, https://chroniclingamerica.loc.gov/lccn/sn86086067/1911-08-17/ed-1/seq-7.

2. "Make Down-River Trip Via Baraboo."

3. Christine Terhune Herrick, "Camping Out," *Watertown Republican*, June 1, 1904, https://chroniclingamerica.loc.gov/lccn/sn85033295/1904-06-01/ed-1/seq-8.

4. "Want Camping Sites: Every Village and City in North Part of State Should Establish Accommodations for Tourists," *Vilas County News*, February 11, 1920, https://chroniclingamerica.loc.gov/lccn/sn85040613/1920-02-11/ed-1/seq-1/.

5. Herrick, "Camping Out."

6. "Make Down-River Trip Via Baraboo."

7. "For Camping Party," *Wausau Pilot*, October 3, 1911, https://chroniclingamerica.loc.gov/lccn/sn85040749/1911-10-03/ed-1/seq-8/.

## All in the Name of Health

1. "Tonic Values of Vegetables," *Eagle River Review*, January 31, 1901, https://chroniclingamerica.loc.gov/lccn/sn85040614/1901-01-31/ed-1/seq-5/.

2. Dariush Mozaffarian, Irwin Rosenberg, and Ricardo Uauy, "History of Modern Nutrition Science—Implications for Current Research, Dietary Guidelines, and Food Policy," *BMJ* 361:k2392 (June 13, 2018), www.bmj.com/content/361/bmj.k2392.

3. Carole Davis and Etta Saltos, "Dietary Recommendations and How They Have Changed over Time," America's Eating Habits: Changes and Consequences, US Department of Agriculture, Economic Research Service, Food and Rural Economics Division, Agriculture Information Bulletin No. 750, 33, May 1999, www.ers.usda.gov/webdocs/publications/42215/5831_aib750b_1_.pdf.

4. "Find Malnutrition Menaces the Nation," *Vilas County News*, August 27, 1924, https://chroniclingamerica.loc.gov/lccn/sn85040613/1924-08-27/ed-1/seq-3/.

5. "Nervous People," *Telegraph-Courier* (Kenosha), March 9, 1899, https://chroniclingamerica.loc.gov/lccn/sn85040310/1899-03-09/ed-1/seq-3/.

6. *Telegraph-Courier* (Kenosha), November 5, 1903, https://chroniclingamerica.loc.gov/lccn/sn85040310/1903-11-05/ed-1/seq-6/.

7. *Baraboo News*, October 28, 1909, https://chroniclingamerica.loc.gov/lccn/sn86086067/1909-10-28/ed-1/seq-3/.

8. "Do We Need a MILK Wave?" *Northern Wisconsin Advertiser* (Wabeno), August 11, 1922, https://chroniclingamerica.loc.gov/lccn/sn85040705/1922-08-11/ed-1/seq-8/.

9. "Successful Milk Campaign," *Washburn Times*, April 7, 1921, https://chroniclingamerica.loc.gov/lccn/sn85040437/1921-04-07/ed-1/seq-6/.

10. "Salads That Tempt," *Watertown Leader*, August 4, 1911, https://chroniclingamerica.loc.gov/lccn/sn85040722/1911-08-04/ed-1/seq-2/.

## Landreth's Legacy

1. "Pass the Peas, Please: Wisconsin's Canning History," Recollection Wisconsin, October 21, 2019, https://recollectionwisconsin.org/canning.

2. *Manitowoc Pilot,* November 22, 1894, https://chroniclingamerica.loc.gov/lccn/sn85033139/1894-11-22/ed-1/seq-3/.

3. Timothy Eggen, "History of Lakeside Packing Company 1887–1987: A Century of Quality," Manitowoc Historical Society, Occupational Monograph 62, 1987.

4. "Among Farmers," *Manitowoc Pilot,* June 27, 1895, https://chroniclingamerica.loc.gov/lccn/sn85033139/1895-06-27/ed-1/seq-2/.

5. *Manitowoc Pilot,* March 3, 1887, https://chroniclingamerica.loc.gov/lccn/sn85033139/1887-03-03/ed-1/seq-3/.

6. *Manitowoc Pilot,* October 29, 1885, https://chroniclingamerica.loc.gov/lccn/sn85033139/1885-10-29/ed-1/seq-3/.

7. "Among Farmers," *Manitowoc Pilot,* August 10, 1893, https://chroniclingamerica.loc.gov/lccn/sn85033139/1893-08-10/ed-1/seq-3/.

8. "Pass the Peas, Please."

9. "Pass the Peas, Please."

10. "Warm Weather Recipes," *Odanah Star*, August 16, 1912, https://chroniclingamerica.loc.gov/lccn/sn84024927/1912-08-16/ed-1/seq-7/.

## Nellie Maxwell

1. " 'Eat and Enjoy It' Is Motto of This Expert," *Ely Miner* (Ely, Minnesota), December 12, 1930, https://chroniclingamerica.loc.gov/lccn/sn90059182/1930-12-12/ed-1/seq-5.

2. "Maxwell, Nellie," *Wisconsin Necrology*, vol. 37, reel no. 5 (Wisconsin Historical Society), 155.

3. "Nellie Maxwell Dies Suddenly," *Antigo Daily Journal*, August 17, 1936.

4. " 'Eat and Enjoy It' Is Motto of This Expert."

5. "For Perfect Jelly," *Ekalaka Eagle* (Ekalaka, Montana), August 20, 1909, https://chroniclingamerica.loc.gov/lccn/sn85053090/1909-08-20/ed-1/seq-7; "Best for Summer," (*Chickasha Daily Express* [Chickasha, Indian Territory [Oklahoma]), August 27, 1909, https://chroniclingamerica.loc.gov/lccn/sn86090528/1909-08-27/ed-1/seq-3.

6. "Nellie Maxwell Dies Suddenly."

7. "Timely Tips for the Housewife: What to Do with Sour Cream," *Ladysmith News-Budget*, July 16, 1915, https://chroniclingamerica.loc.gov/lccn/sn85040245/1915-07-16/ed-1/seq-6.

## Wisconsin Goes Bananas

1. "The Banana Tree," *Grant County Herald*, August 26, 1862, https://chroniclingamerica.loc.gov/lccn/sn85033133/1862-08-26/ed-1/seq-1.

2. "The Latest Telegrams," *Iowa County Democrat*, November 21, 1890, https://chroniclingamerica.loc.gov/lccn/sn86086852/1890-11-21/ed-1/seq-1.

3. "Stepped on a Banana Peeling," *Wisconsin Tobacco Reporter* (Edgerton), August 9, 1901, https://chroniclingamerica.loc.gov/lccn/sn86086586/1901-08-09/ed-1/seq-2.

4. *Kenosha Telegraph*, April 13, 1871, https://chroniclingamerica.loc.gov/lccn/sn85033123/1871-04-13/ed-1/seq-8; "Dressed Bananas," *Wood County Reporter*, June 18, 1874, https://chroniclingamerica.loc.gov/lccn/sn85033078/1874-06-18/ed-1/seq-6.

5. *Grant County Herald*, December 11, 1912, https://chroniclingamerica.loc.gov/lccn/sn85033133/1912-12-11/ed-1/seq-3/.

6. "For Those Fond of Salads," *Mineral Point Tribune*, December 14, 1916, https://chroniclingamerica.loc.gov/lccn/sn86086770/1916-12-14/ed-1/seq-7/.

# The Cherry on Top

**1.** "Maraschino Cherries," *Eagle River Review*, August 6, 1909, https://chroniclingamerica.loc.gov/lccn/sn85040614/1909-08-06/ed-1/seq-4/.

**2.** "Adieu to Maraschino," *Manitowoc Pilot*, July 12, 1906, https://chroniclingamerica.loc.gov/lccn/sn85033139/1906-07-12/ed-1/seq-2.

**3.** US Food and Drug Administration, *Maraschino Cherries*, Center for Food Safety and Applied Nutrition, Office of Regulatory Affairs, Compliance Policy Guide Sec 550.550, 1980, www.fda.gov/regulatory-information/search-fda-guidance-documents/cpg-sec-550550-maraschino-cherries.

**4.** Inara Verzemnieks, "Maraschino Cherries," *Oregon Encyclopedia*, June 7, 2022, www.oregonencyclopedia.org/articles/maraschino_cherries/.

**5.** US Food and Drug Administration, *Maraschino Cherries*.

**6.** "The Kitchen Cabinet," *Northern Wisconsin Advertiser* (Wabeno), December 16, 1910, https://chroniclingamerica.loc.gov/lccn/sn85040705/1910-12-16/ed-1/seq-3/.

# Measurements and Standardization

**1.** Fannie Merritt Farmer, *The Boston Cooking-School Cook Book* (Boston: Little, Brown, and Company, 1896), 27.

**2.** "Facts in Cooking," *Eagle River Review*, May 5, 1898, https://chroniclingamerica.loc.gov/lccn/sn85040614/1898-05-05/ed-1/seq-5/.

**3.** "An Economical Fruit Cake," *Vilas County News*, August 9, 1911, https://chroniclingamerica.loc.gov/lccn/sn85040613/1911-08-09/ed-1/seq-7.

**4.** "Hot Chocolate," *Wauwatosa News*, December 14, 1917, https://chroniclingamerica.loc.gov/lccn/sn86086499/1917-12-14/ed-1/seq-2/.

**5.** US Const. Art. I, Sect. 8, Cl. 5.

**6.** Danielle Dreilinger, *The Secret History of Home Economics: How Trailblazing Women Harnessed the Power of Home and Changed the Way We Live* (New York: W. W. Norton & Company, 2021), 66.

**7.** "Salad for the Summer," *Northern Wisconsin Advertiser* (Wabeno), August 8, 1907, https://chroniclingamerica.loc.gov/lccn/sn85040705/1907-08-08/ed-1/seq-4/.

# Mixing It Up

**1.** W. W. Lyman, Can Opener, US Patent 105346A, issued July 12, 1870, https://patents.google.com/patent/US105346A/en; L. T. Snow, Food Chopper, US Patent 591575A, issued October 12, 1897, https://patents.google.com/patent/US591575A/en.

**2.** R. Collier, Egg-Beater, US Patent 16267A, issued December 23, 1856, https://patents.google.com/patent/US16267A/en.

3. J. F. and E. P. Monroe, Egg-Beater, US Patent 23694A, issued April 19, 1859, https://patents.google.com/patent/US23694A/en.

4. *Telegraph-Courier* (Kenosha), September 2, 1915, https://chroniclingamerica.loc.gov/lccn/sn85040310/1915-09-02/ed-1/seq-8/.

5. " 'Portable' Egg-Beater," *Eagle River Review*, September 20, 1900, https://chroniclingamerica.loc.gov/lccn/sn85040614/1900-09-20/ed-1/seq-5/.

6. "Effective Egg Beater," *Wauwatosa News*, December 10, 1909, https://chroniclingamerica.loc.gov/lccn/sn86086499/1909-12-10/ed-1/seq-6/.

7. "Effective Egg Beater."

8. "Interesting New Inventions: Electricity Beats Eggs," *Grant County Herald*, September 9, 1908, https://chroniclingamerica.loc.gov/lccn/sn85033133/1908-09-09/ed-1/seq-2/.

9. "The Household," *Watertown Republican*, February 25, 1874, https://chroniclingamerica.loc.gov/lccn/sn85033295/1874-02-25/ed-1/seq-3/.

## Hot and Quick or Cool and Slow

1. "Recipe for Making Corn Bread," *Prescott Journal*, February 9, 1867, https://chroniclingamerica.loc.gov/lccn/sn85033221/1867-02-09/ed-1/seq-3/.

2. "Oven Temperature for Cake," *Washburn Times*, November 6, 1902, https://chroniclingamerica.loc.gov/lccn/sn85040437/1902-11-06/ed-1/seq-6.

3. "Baking Bread," *Wood County Reporter*, August 14, 1884, https://chroniclingamerica.loc.gov/lccn/sn85033078/1884-08-14/ed-1/seq-8.

4. "How to Test an Oven before You Burn Your Cake," *Wausau Pilot,* April 4, 1916, https://chroniclingamerica.loc.gov/lccn/sn85040749/1916-04-04/ed-1/seq-5.

5. "Heat in the Oven," *Eagle River Review*, February 21, 1903, https://chroniclingamerica.loc.gov/lccn/sn85040614/1903-02-21/ed-1/seq-4/.

6. "Temperature of Oven Important," *Manitowoc Pilot*, January 5, 1922, https://chroniclingamerica.loc.gov/lccn/sn85033139/1922-01-05/ed-1/seq-7/.

7. "Temperature of Oven Important."

8. "Food Preparations and Thermometers," *Eagle River Review*, July 23, 1925, https://chroniclingamerica.loc.gov/lccn/sn85040614/1925-07-23/ed-1/seq-8/.

9. "SI Units: Temperature," National Institute of Standards and Technology Physical Measurements Laboratory, November 8, 2022, www.nist.gov/pml/owm/si-units-temperature.

10. "Farm and Household," *Dodgeville Chronicle*, May 16, 1873, https://chroniclingamerica.loc.gov/lccn/sn85033019/1873-05-16/ed-1/seq-4/.

# The Many Faces of Sourdough

1. Jack London, "Burning Daylight," *Ladysmith News-Budget*, May 17, 1912, https://chroniclingamerica.loc.gov/lccn/sn85040245/1912-05-17/ed-1/seq-6.

2. "Alaskan Pioneers Cared For," *Eagle River Review*, May 9, 1919, https://chroniclingamerica.loc.gov/lccn/sn85040614/1919-05-09/ed-1/seq-2/.

3. "Die Sozialdemokraten in Deutschland [Social Democrats in Germany]," *Der Sonntagsbote* (Milwaukee), April 5, 1908, https://chroniclingamerica.loc.gov/lccn/sn87082455/1908-04-05/ed-1/seq-4.

4. "Bischof v. Ketteler und die sociale Frage [Bischof v. Ketteler and the Social Question]," *Der Sonnatgsbote*, December 24, 1911, https://chroniclingamerica.loc.gov/lccn/sn87082455/1911-12-24/ed-1/seq-5.

5. "Beamte [Officers]," *Nord Stern* (La Crosse), March 26, 1909, https://chroniclingamerica.loc.gov/lccn/sn86086186/1909-03-26/ed-1/seq-8/.

6. "Briefkasten des Landraths [District Counsel Mailbox]," *Nord Stern* (La Crosse), December 22, 1916, https://chroniclingamerica.loc.gov/lccn/sn86086186/1916-12-22/ed-1/seq-7/.

# Between Two Slices of Bread

1. "Sandwiches," *Grant County Herald*, August 6, 1867, https://chroniclingamerica.loc.gov/lccn/sn85033133/1867-08-06/ed-1/seq-2/.

2. "How to Make Good Sandwiches," *Mineral Point Tribune*, May 28, 1892, https://chroniclingamerica.loc.gov/lccn/sn86086770/1892-05-28/ed-1/seq-3/.

3. "Season of Sandwiches," *Mineral Point Tribune*, August 12, 1893, https://chroniclingamerica.loc.gov/lccn/sn86086770/1893-08-12/ed-1/seq-6/.

4. "Sandwiches for Summer Days," *Vernon County Censor*, June 27, 1906, https://chroniclingamerica.loc.gov/lccn/sn85040451/1906-06-27/ed-1/seq-2/.

5. Kat Eschner, "Take a Look at the Patents Behind Sliced Bread," *Smithsonian Magazine*, July 7, 2017, www.smithsonianmag.com/smart-news/take-look-patents-behind-sliced-bread-180963870/.

6. Rhonda Sebastian, Cecilia Wilkinson Enns, Joseph Goldman, Mary Katherine Hoy, and Alanna Moshfegh, *Sandwich Consumption by Adults in the US: What We Eat in America NHANES 2009–2012*. USDA Agricultural Research Service, Food Surveys Research Group Dietary Data Brief no. 14, December 2015, www.ncbi.nlm.nih.gov/books/NBK589471/.

7. "A Collection of Sandwiches," *Manitowoc Pilot*, September 5, 1912, https://chroniclingamerica.loc.gov/lccn/sn85033139/1912-09-05/ed-1/seq-6/.

## Keeping Things Fresh

1. "Of Interest to the Housewife," *Wauwatosa News*, August 25, 1922, https://chroniclingamerica.loc.gov/lccn/sn86086499/1922-08-25/ed-1/seq-7/.

2. "Points on Kitchen Economy," *Vernon County Censor*, October 25, 1916, https://chroniclingamerica.loc.gov/lccn/sn85040451/1916-10-25/ed-1/seq-2/.

3. "For Women and Girls," *Eagle River Review*, May 7, 1909, https://chroniclingamerica.loc.gov/lccn/sn85040614/1909-05-07/ed-1/seq-7/.

4. "The Housewife's Exchange," *Wausau Pilot*, June 15, 1922, https://chroniclingamerica.loc.gov/lccn/sn85040749/1922-06-15/ed-1/seq-2/.

## The Commercialization of Cheese

1. "Agricultural," *Southport Telegraph* (Kenosha), July 13, 1842, https://chroniclingamerica.loc.gov/lccn/sn85040303/1842-07-13/ed-1/seq-1/.

2. "Dairy Farming in Wisconsin: How Wisconsin Became the Dairy State," Wisconsin Historical Society, www.wisconsinhistory.org/Records/Article/CS1744#:~:text=Wisconsin%20did%20not%20start%20out,farmers%20take%20up%20dairy%20farming.

3. "Cheese Factories," *Kenosha Telegraph*, August 4, 1864, https://chroniclingamerica.loc.gov/lccn/sn85033123/1864-08-04/ed-1/seq-4/.

4. "Domestic Paragraphs," *Dodgeville Chronicle*, November 15, 1866, https://chroniclingamerica.loc.gov/lccn/sn85033019/1866-11-15/ed-1/seq-3/.

5. "Miscellaneous Items," *Mineral Point Tribune*, March 17, 1869, https://chroniclingamerica.loc.gov/lccn/sn86086770/1869-03-17/ed-1/seq-1/.

6. "Some Things to Crow About," *Iowa County Democrat*, July 15, 1915, https://chroniclingamerica.loc.gov/lccn/sn86086852/1915-07-15/ed-1/seq-3/; "Wisconsin Leads All," *Vilas County News*, September 5, 1923, https://chroniclingamerica.loc.gov/lccn/sn85040613/1923-09-05/ed-1/seq-5/.

7. "The Housewife's Exchange," *Wausau Pilot*, June 29, 1922, https://chroniclingamerica.loc.gov/lccn/sn85040749/1922-06-29/ed-1/seq-2/.

## Planning and Planting

1. "Home Garden Plan Saves Time, Money, and Labor for Gardener," *Wood County Reporter*, April 25, 1918, https://chroniclingamerica.loc.gov/lccn/sn85033078/1918-04-25/ed-1/seq-6/.

2. "Don't Neglect the Garden," *Eagle River Review*, June 13, 1919, https://chroniclingamerica.loc.gov/lccn/sn85040614/1919-06-13/ed-1/seq-5/.

3. "Grow Own Table Dainties," *Washburn Times*, November 2, 1911, https://chroniclingamerica.loc.gov/lccn/sn85040437/1911-11-02/ed-1/seq-8/.

4. "Squashes in Home Gardens," *Washburn Times*, April 20, 1922, https://chroniclingamerica.loc.gov/lccn/sn85040437/1922-04-20/ed-1/seq-5/.

5. "New Recipe for Cooking Squash," *Wauwatosa News*, January 10, 1908, https://chroniclingamerica.loc.gov/lccn/sn86086499/1908-01-10/ed-1/seq-3/.

## A Historical Storage Solution

1. "Find Your Wants Here," *Vernon County Censor*, September 14, 1921, https://chroniclingamerica.loc.gov/lccn/sn85040451/1921-09-14/ed-1/seq-8/.

2. *Ladysmith News-Budget*, April 22, 1909, https://chroniclingamerica.loc.gov/lccn/sn85040245/1909-04-22/ed-1/seq-7/.

3. "Energy Saver 101 History Timeline: Refrigeration and Refrigerators," US Department of Energy, n.d., www.energy.gov/energysaver/energy-saver-101-history-timeline-refrigeration-and-refrigerators.

4. "Problem of Winter Vegetable Storage," *Northern Wisconsin Advertiser* (Wabeno), November 10, 1916, https://chroniclingamerica.loc.gov/lccn/sn85040705/1916-11-10/ed-1/seq-7/.

5. "Ways of Using Cottage Cheese," *Iowa County Democrat*, November 21, 1918, https://chroniclingamerica.loc.gov/lccn/sn86086852/1918-11-21/ed-1/seq-7/.

## Helpful Hints and Crop Reports

1. "Helpful Hints for Our Modern Farmers," *Eagle River Review*, June 7, 1923, https://chroniclingamerica.loc.gov/lccn/sn85040614/1923-06-07/ed-1/seq-5/.

2. Carole Scott, "The History of the Radio Industry in the United States to 1940," EH.Net Encyclopedia, March 26, 2008, https://eh.net/encyclopedia/the-history-of-the-radio-industry-in-the-united-states-to-1940/.

3. "Our Part in Feeding the Nation," *Washburn Times*, July 25, 1918, https://chroniclingamerica.loc.gov/lccn/sn85040437/1918-07-25/ed-1/seq-6/.

4. "Potatoes Foremost among Vegetables," *Eagle River Review*, October 11, 1923, https://chroniclingamerica.loc.gov/lccn/sn85040614/1923-10-11/ed-1/seq-5/; "Our Part in Feeding the Nation."

5. "The Kitchen Cupboard: Spinach Suggestions," *Our Land–La Nostra Terra* (Hurley), August 30, 1913, https://chroniclingamerica.loc.gov/lccn/sn85040651/1913-08-30/ed-1/seq-6/.

## Meatless Mincemeat and Poultry Exceptions

1. Spencer Colin, foreword to *A Heretic's Feast: A History of Vegetarianism* (Hanover, NH: University Press of New England, 1995), ix.

2. *Baraboo News*, February 7, 1906, https://chroniclingamerica.loc.gov/lccn/sn86086067/1906-02-07/ed-1/seq-4/.

3. "Missing Links," *Wood County Reporter*, April 16, 1885, https://chroniclingamerica.loc.gov/lccn/sn85033078/1885-04-16/ed-1/seq-8/.

4. "No More Vegetarian Restaurant," *Manitowoc Pilot*, November 21, 1895, https://chroniclingamerica.loc.gov/lccn/sn85033139/1895-11-21/ed-1/seq-4/.

5. "Meatless Diet Healthful," *River Falls Journal*, August 25, 1904, https://chroniclingamerica.loc.gov/lccn/sn85033255/1904-08-25/ed-1/seq-6/.

6. "A Leaf for the Vegetarians," *Grant County Herald*, November 13, 1854, https://chroniclingamerica.loc.gov/lccn/sn85033133/1854-11-13/ed-1/seq-1/.

7. "Uncle Sam Intends to Protect Your Soldier Boy from Booze and the 'Great Red Plague,'" *Eagle River Review*, July 20, 1917, https://chroniclingamerica.loc.gov/lccn/sn85040614/1917-07-20/ed-1/seq-6/.

8. "Rigid Inspection of Meat Certain under New Rules," *River Falls Journal*, August 2, 1906, https://chroniclingamerica.loc.gov/lccn/sn85033255/1906-08-02/ed-1/seq-3/.

9. "What Women Are Doing," *Northern Wisconsin Advertiser* (Wabeno), August 23, 1906, https://chroniclingamerica.loc.gov/lccn/sn85040705/1906-08-23/ed-1/seq-7/.

10. "Hints for the Busy Housewife," *Iowa County Democrat*, November 30, 1911, https://chroniclingamerica.loc.gov/lccn/sn86086852/1911-11-30/ed-1/seq-6/.

11. "Find No Cut in Cold Storage Poultry Held," *Baraboo Weekly News*, December 20, 1917, https://chroniclingamerica.loc.gov/lccn/sn86086068/1917-12-20/ed-1/seq-2/.

12. "Timely Tips for the Housewife," *River Falls Journal*, June 3, 1915, https://chroniclingamerica.loc.gov/lccn/sn85033255/1915-06-03/ed-1/seq-1/; "Meatless Bean Soup," *Eagle River Review*, May 27, 1897, https://chroniclingamerica.loc.gov/lccn/sn85040614/1897-05-27/ed-1/seq-5/.

13. "Cowpeas Quite Good as Meat Substitute," *Northern Wisconsin Advertiser* (Wabeno), February 11, 1921, https://chroniclingamerica.loc.gov/lccn/sn85040705/1921-02-11/ed-1/seq-7/.

## Paper Bag Cooking

1. *Washburn Times*, February 22, 1912, https://chroniclingamerica.loc.gov/lccn/sn85040437/1912-02-22/ed-1/seq-6/.

2. Nicolas Soyer, *Soyer's Paper-Bag Cookery* (United Kingdom: Sturgis & Walton Company, 1911), Internet Archive, https://archive.org/details/soyerspaperbagc00soyegoog/page/n16/mode/2up.

3. Soyer, *Soyer's Paper-Bag Cookery*, 8.

4. "Paper Bag Cookery," *Watertown Leader*, October 27, 1911, https://chroniclingamerica.loc.gov/lccn/sn85040722/1911-10-27/ed-1/seq-3.

5. "Paper Bag Cooking," *Wisconsin Tobacco Reporter* (Edgerton), November 24, 1911, https://chroniclingamerica.loc.gov/lccn/sn86086586/1911-11-24/ed-1/seq-4/; Martha McCulloch Williams, "Paper Bag Cooking: Wonder-Working System Perfected by M. Soyer, World's Greatest Living Chef," *Northern Wisconsin Advertiser* (Wabeno), March 29, 1912, https://chroniclingamerica.loc.gov/lccn/sn85040705/1912-03-29/ed-1/seq-3/.

6. "To Give Demonstration," *Watertown Weekly Leader*, May 3, 1912, https://chroniclingamerica.loc.gov/lccn/sn85040721/1912-05-03/ed-1/seq-1/.

7. *Washburn Times*, December 14, 1911, https://chroniclingamerica.loc.gov/lccn/sn85040437/1911-12-14/ed-1/seq-7/.

8. "The Lazy Way," *Wood County Reporter*, July 10, 1913, https://chroniclingamerica.loc.gov/lccn/sn85033078/1913-07-10/ed-1/seq-2/.

9. "All Worth While: Every Kind of Fad Has Some Advantage," *Vernon County Censor*, February 7, 1917, https://chroniclingamerica.loc.gov/lccn/sn85040451/1917-02-07/ed-1/seq-2/.

10. "The Kitchen Cabinet," *Manitowoc Pilot*, November 21, 1912, https://chroniclingamerica.loc.gov/lccn/sn85033139/1912-11-21/ed-1/seq-7/.

## Wired with Excitement

1. *Kenosha Telegraph*, October 31, 1878, https://chroniclingamerica.loc.gov/lccn/sn85033123/1878-10-31/ed-1/seq-3/.

2. "News about Electricity," *Watertown Republican*, July 23, 1890, https://chroniclingamerica.loc.gov/lccn/sn85033295/1890-07-23/ed-1/seq-7/.

3. "Heating by Electricity," *Watertown Republican*, April 5, 1893, https://chroniclingamerica.loc.gov/lccn/sn85033295/1893-04-05/ed-1/seq-6/.

4. "Lightning Cookery," *Eagle River Review*, March 29, 1894, https://chroniclingamerica.loc.gov/lccn/sn85040614/1894-03-29/ed-1/seq-1/.

5. "News about Electricity."

6. "Fair Notes," *Superior Times*, October 29, 1892, https://chroniclingamerica.loc.gov/lccn/sn85040344/1892-10-29/ed-1/seq-5/.

7. *Wood County Reporter*, May 25, 1911, https://chroniclingamerica.loc.gov/lccn/sn85033078/1911-05-25/ed-1/seq-5/.

8. *Wisconsin Tobacco Reporter* (Edgerton), May 30, 1919, https://chroniclingamerica.loc.gov/lccn/sn86086586/1919-05-30/ed-1/seq-7/.

9. "Home Cookery," *Wisconsin Weekly Blade* (Madison), September 7, 1916, https://chroniclingamerica.loc.gov/lccn/sn84025842/1916-09-07/ed-1/seq-1/.

## For the Love of Pasta

1. "Boiled Macaroni," *Watertown Republican,* September 23, 1891, https://chroniclingamerica.loc.gov/lccn/sn85033295/1891-09-23/ed-1/seq-6.

2. "Time of Cooking," *Wood County Reporter,* April 28, 1898, https://chroniclingamerica.loc.gov/lccn/sn85033078/1898-04-28/ed-1/seq-2/; "Time Table," *Eagle River Review,* September 27, 1900, https://chroniclingamerica.loc.gov/lccn/sn85040614/1900-09-27/ed-1/seq-5/.

3. *Kenosha Telegraph,* October 11, 1850, https://chroniclingamerica.loc.gov/lccn/sn85040305/1850-10-11/ed-1/seq-2.

4. "The Kitchen Cabinet," *Watertown Weekly Leader,* February 16, 1915, https://chroniclingamerica.loc.gov/lccn/sn85040721/1915-02-16/ed-1/seq-3/.

## (Un)pleasing to the Eye

1. Horan Engraving, "The Art and Technique of Photoengraving," ca. 1950s, available at https://vimeo.com/134626010.

2. "Discovery in Photography. Steel Engraving Effects Produced by a New Process," *Wood County Reporter,* February 6, 1896, https://chroniclingamerica.loc.gov/lccn/sn85033078/1896-02-06/ed-1/seq-3.

3. *Telegraph-Courier* (Kenosha), May 29, 1890, https://chroniclingamerica.loc.gov/lccn/sn85040310/1890-05-29/ed-2/seq-1.

4. "The Young Bride's Housekeeping," *Vernon County Censor,* August 25, 1909, https://chroniclingamerica.loc.gov/lccn/sn85040451/1909-08-25/ed-1/seq-3/.

## Historical Clean Eating

1. John W Parry, "The Story of Spices," *Economic Botany* 9, no. 2 (April–June 1955): 190, www.jstor.org/stable/4287851.

2. "Hygienic Menus," *Kenosha Telegraph,* April 8, 1881, https://chroniclingamerica.loc.gov/lccn/sn85033123/1881-04-08/ed-1/seq-1/.

3. *Wood County Reporter,* May 28, 1874, https://chroniclingamerica.loc.gov/lccn/sn85033078/1874-05-28/ed-1/seq-3.

4. "Health and Beauty Hints," *Wausau Pilot,* February 4, 1908, https://chroniclingamerica.loc.gov/lccn/sn85040749/1908-02-04/ed-1/seq-7/; "Woman's World: Proper Diet for the Thin and Nervous," *Iowa County Democrat,* May 25, 1905, https://chroniclingamerica.loc.gov/lccn/sn86086852/1905-05-25/ed-1/seq-3.

5. "Children's Diet, Good and Bad," *Kenosha Telegraph,* December 29, 1882, https://chroniclingamerica.loc.gov/lccn/sn85033123/1882-12-29/ed-1/seq-4.

6. Vern L. Bullough, "Technology for the Prevention of 'Les Maladies Produites par la Masturbation,'" *Technology and Culture* 28, no. 4 (October 1987): 829, www.jstor.org/stable/3105184.

7. Dr. J. H. Hanaford, "Temperance Reading: Harmful Cookery," *Kenosha Telegraph*, August 10, 1888, https://chroniclingamerica.loc.gov/lccn/sn85033123/1888-08-10/ed-1/seq-4/.

8. "The Housewife's Exchange," *Wausau Pilot*, July 6, 1922, https://chroniclingamerica.loc.gov/lccn/sn85040749/1922-07-06/ed-1/seq-2.

## Sharing Local Recipes

1. "The Housewife's Exchange," *Wausau Pilot*, June 15, 1922, https://chroniclingamerica.loc.gov/lccn/sn85040749/1922-06-15/ed-1/seq-2.

2. "The Housewife's Help," *Wausau Pilot*, June 15, 1922, https://chroniclingamerica.loc.gov/lccn/sn85040749/1922-06-15/ed-1/seq-1.

3. "The Housewife's Exchange," *Wausau Pilot*, June 15, 1922, https://chroniclingamerica.loc.gov/lccn/sn85040749/1922-06-15/ed-1/seq-2.

4. "The Housewife's Exchange," *Wausau Pilot*, December 14, 1922, https://chroniclingamerica.loc.gov/lccn/sn85040749/1922-12-14/ed-1/seq-8; "The Housewife's Exchange," *Wausau Pilot*, June 15, 1922, https://chroniclingamerica.loc.gov/lccn/sn85040749/1922-06-15/ed-1/seq-2; "The Housewife's Exchange," *Wausau Pilot*, July 13, 1922, https://chroniclingamerica.loc.gov/lccn/sn85040749/1922-07-13/ed-1/seq-2/; "The Housewife's Exchange," *Wausau Pilot*, October 12, 1922, https://chroniclingamerica.loc.gov/lccn/sn85040749/1922-10-12/ed-1/seq-2/.

5. "The Housewife's Exchange," *Wausau Pilot*, July 13, 1922, https://chroniclingamerica.loc.gov/lccn/sn85040749/1922-07-13/ed-1/seq-2/.

## Mr. Smith Went Fishing Last Saturday

1. "Neighborhood News," *River Falls Journal*, September 11, 1902, https://chroniclingamerica.loc.gov/lccn/sn85033255/1902-09-11/ed-1/seq-4/.

2. "News of Kenosha County," *Telegraph-Courier* (Kenosha), September 30, 1915, https://chroniclingamerica.loc.gov/lccn/sn85040310/1915-09-30/ed-1/seq-5/; "Personals." *Wood County Reporter*, August 28, 1890, https://chroniclingamerica.loc.gov/lccn/sn85033078/1890-08-28/ed-1/seq-1/.

3. "Monday," *Baraboo Weekly News*, June 4, 1914, https://chroniclingamerica.loc.gov/lccn/sn86086068/1914-06-04/ed-1/seq-9/.

4. "For Camping Party," *Wausau Pilot*, October 3, 1911, https://chroniclingamerica.loc.gov/lccn/sn85040749/1911-10-03/ed-1/seq-8/.

## Waste Not, Want Not

1. "Plenty of Material," *Vilas County News*, June 5, 1912, https://chroniclingamerica.loc.gov/lccn/sn85040613/1912-06-05/ed-1/seq-2/.

2. "American Extravagance in Living," *Dodgeville Chronicle*, August 10, 1865, https://chroniclingamerica.loc.gov/lccn/sn85033019/1865-08-10/ed-1/seq-1/.

3. "Serving at Table," *Kenosha Telegraph*, December 14, 1871, https://chroniclingamerica.loc.gov/lccn/sn85033123/1871-12-14/ed-1/seq-6/.

4. "Will Hunger Come?" *Iron County News*, May 12, 1917, https://chroniclingamerica.loc.gov/lccn/sn85040652/1917-05-12/ed-1/seq-1/.

5. "Careful Selection of Food for Table," *Eagle River Review*, June 21, 1923, https://chroniclingamerica.loc.gov/lccn/sn85040614/1923-06-21/ed-1/seq-8/.

6. Nellie Maxwell, "A Day with Leftovers," *Wood County Reporter*, December 16, 1915, https://chroniclingamerica.loc.gov/lccn/sn85033078/1915-12-16/ed-1/seq-2/; "Use for 'Left-Overs,'" *Vernon County Censor*, March 31, 1915, https://chroniclingamerica.loc.gov/lccn/sn85040451/1915-03-31/ed-1/seq-2/.

7. "Proper Care of Food Will Prevent Waste," *Eagle River Review*, February 21, 1924, https://chroniclingamerica.loc.gov/lccn/sn85040614/1924-02-21/ed-1/seq-8/.

8. "Ice Economy!" *Baraboo Weekly News*, June 26, 1924, https://chroniclingamerica.loc.gov/lccn/sn86086068/1924-06-26/ed-1/seq-2/.

9. Dora Rude, "To the Women of Iron County," *Iron County News*, April 27, 1918, https://chroniclingamerica.loc.gov/lccn/sn85040652/1918-04-27/ed-1/seq-4/.

10. "The Kitchen Cupboard," *Our Land–La Nostra Terra* (Hurley), July 5, 1913, https://chroniclingamerica.loc.gov/lccn/sn85040651/1913-07-05/ed-1/seq-5.

## Shipped on Ice

1. *Wisconsin Tribune* (Mineral Point), February 1, 1850, https://chroniclingamerica.loc.gov/lccn/sn86086768/1850-02-01/ed-1/seq-3/.

2. *Tribune and Telegraph* (Kenosha), January 3, 1856, https://chroniclingamerica.loc.gov/lccn/sn85040307/1856-01-03/ed-1/seq-2/.

3. "Lovers of Lobster," *Wood County Reporter*, November 14, 1889, https://chroniclingamerica.loc.gov/lccn/sn85033078/1889-11-14/ed-1/seq-5/.

4. "Live Lobsters in Demand," *Wood County Reporter*, July 9, 1891, https://chroniclingamerica.loc.gov/lccn/sn85033078/1891-07-09/ed-1/seq-4/.

5. "Lobster a La Newburg," *Wausau Pilot*, November 14, 1911, https://chroniclingamerica.loc.gov/lccn/sn85040749/1911-11-14/ed-1/seq-2/.

## Briny with a Cult Following

**1.** *Southport Telegraph* (Kenosha), November 30, 1842, https://chroniclingamerica.loc.gov/lccn/sn85040303/1842-11-30/ed-1/seq-3/.

**2.** "Arthur E. Stilwell," Pullman History Site, April 2020, www.pullman-museum.org/theCompany/stillwell.html.

**3.** "The Criminal Calendar," *Manitowoc Pilot*, October 25, 1877, h ttps://chroniclingamerica.loc.gov/lccn/sn85033139/1877-10-25/ed-1/seq-1/.

**4.** *Mineral Point Weekly Tribune*, January 23, 1867, https://chroniclingamerica.loc.gov/lccn/sn86086769/1867-01-23/ed-1/seq-1/.

**5.** "Domestic Concerns," *River Falls Journal*, February 4, 1892, https://chroniclingamerica.loc.gov/lccn/sn85033255/1892-02-04/ed-1/seq-3/; "The Household," *Manitowoc Pilot*, January 31, 1878, https://chroniclingamerica.loc.gov/lccn/sn85033139/1878-01-31/ed-1/seq-4.

**6.** "Farm and Home," *Mineral Point Tribune*, June 5, 1878, https://chroniclingamerica.loc.gov/lccn/sn86086770/1878-06-05/ed-1/seq-7/.

## In the Old Sugarbush

**1.** "Sugar Making in the Maple Wood," *Wauwatosa News*, March 19, 1915, https://chroniclingamerica.loc.gov/lccn/sn86086499/1915-03-19/ed-1/seq-2/.

**2.** "Maple Syrup Industry," Wisconsin Historical Society, https://wisconsinhistory.org/Records/Article/CS1821.

**3.** Matthew M. Thomas, "Reynolds Sugar Bush: Putting Wisconsin on the Maple Syrup Map," *Wisconsin Magazine of History* 105, no. 3 (Spring 2022): 44.

**4.** E. A. Bushnell, "Delights of the Maple Sugar Season," *Wausau Pilot*, March 3, 1903, https://chroniclingamerica.loc.gov/lccn/sn85040749/1903-03-03/ed-1/seq-3/.

**5.** Heid E. Erdrich, *Original Local: Indigenous Foods, Stories, and Recipes from the Upper Midwest*, Minneapolis: Minnesota Historical Society Press, 2013.

**6.** Bushnell, "Delights of the Maple Sugar Season."

## Doing Without

**1.** "Heavy Rain Saves Crops," *Watertown Leader*, August 19, 1910, https://chroniclingamerica.loc.gov/lccn/sn85040722/1910-08-19/ed-1/seq-7.

**2.** "Fight Disease of Bee," *Grant County Herald*, December 19, 1917, https://chroniclingamerica.loc.gov/lccn/sn85033133/1917-12-19/ed-1/seq-14.

**3.** "Sugar Shortage Hits Baraboo," *Baraboo Weekly News*, August 7, 1919, https://chroniclingamerica.loc.gov/lccn/sn86086068/1919-08-07/ed-1/seq-1/.

**4.** "Preserving Fruit without Sugar," *Kenosha Tribune and Telegraph*, September 30, 1858, https://chroniclingamerica.loc.gov/lccn/sn85040308/1858-09-30/ed-1/seq-1.

**5.** "Care of Winter Apples," *Watertown Republican*, November 18, 1903, https://chroniclingamerica.loc.gov/lccn/sn85033295/1903-11-18/ed-1/seq-3/.

**6.** "Mock Cherry Pie," *Iron County News*, December 4, 1915, https://chroniclingamerica.loc.gov/lccn/sn85040652/1915-12-04/ed-1/seq-7; "Mock Cherry Pie," *Watertown Republican*, March 16, 1904, https://chroniclingamerica.loc.gov/lccn/sn85033295/1904-03-16/ed-1/seq-3.

**7.** "Mock Lemon Pie," *Iron County News*, July 22, 1916, https://chroniclingamerica.loc.gov/lccn/sn85040652/1916-07-22/ed-1/seq-7.

**8.** "Mock Venison," *Wauwatosa News*, January 17, 1908, https://chroniclingamerica.loc.gov/lccn/sn86086499/1908-01-17/ed-1/seq-6.

**9.** "Mock Apple Pie," *Mineral Point Tribune*, August 11, 1887, https://chroniclingamerica.loc.gov/lccn/sn86086770/1887-08-11/ed-1/seq-7/.

## A Vindication of the Prune

**1.** "Mother's Cook Book: What to Feed the Child," *Washburn Times*, January 30, 1919, https://chroniclingamerica.loc.gov/lccn/sn85040437/1919-01-30/ed-1/seq-3/.

**2.** "Acceptable Gift," *Washburn Times*, October 31, 1912, https://chroniclingamerica.loc.gov/lccn/sn85040437/1912-10-31/ed-1/seq-7/.

**3.** "Of Interest to the Housewife," *Eagle River Review*, July 5, 1923, https://chroniclingamerica.loc.gov/lccn/sn85040614/1923-07-05/ed-1/seq-8/.

**4.** Andrew F. Currier, "Your Health: Uric Acid Condition," *Eagle River Review*, September 3, 1925, https://chroniclingamerica.loc.gov/lccn/sn85040614/1925-09-03/ed-1/seq-3/.

**5.** *Telegraph-Courier* (Kenosha), February 26, 1891, https://chroniclingamerica.loc.gov/lccn/sn85040310/1891-02-26/ed-1/seq-4/.

**6.** *Baraboo News*, May 6, 1908, https://chroniclingamerica.loc.gov/lccn/sn86086067/1908-05-06/ed-1/seq-6/.

**7.** *Nostrums and Quackery: Articles on the Nostrum Evil and Quackery* (Chicago, IL: Press of American Medical Association, 1911), Internet Archive, https://archive.org/details/nostrumsquackery00amerrich/page/318/mode/2up.

**8.** "Mock Pumpkin Pie," *Iron County News*, April 17, 1915, https://chroniclingamerica.loc.gov/lccn/sn85040652/1915-04-17/ed-1/seq-6/.

## Eating Chocolate

**1.** Amanda Fiegl, "A Brief History of Chocolate," *Smithsonian Magazine*, March 1, 2008, www.smithsonianmag.com/arts-culture/a-brief-history-of-chocolate-21860917.

**2.** Marcia and Frederic Morton, *Chocolate: An Illustrated History* (New York: Crown Publishers, 1986), 47–48.

**3.** "Línea de tiempo del chocolate [Chocolate Timeline]" Uxmal, Mexico: Choco-Story Uxmal, 2022, https://choco-story-uxmal.mx/en/museo.

**4.** Morton, *Chocolate*, 33–34.

**5.** *Telegraph-Courier* (Kenosha), April 21, 1898, https://chroniclingamerica.loc.gov/lccn/sn85040310/1898-04-21/ed-1/seq-7.

**6.** "The Kitchen Cabinet," *Manitowoc Pilot*, November 2, 1922, https://chroniclingamerica.loc.gov/lccn/sn85033139/1922-11-02/ed-1/seq-2/.

**7.** "Original Recipes—From Our Readers," *New-York Tribune*, October 12, 1919, https://chroniclingamerica.loc.gov/lccn/sn83030214/1919-10-12/ed-1/seq-76/.

## Death in Rhubarb Leaves

**1.** "Wins First Prize," *Baraboo Weekly News*, April 25, 1912, https://chroniclingamerica.loc.gov/lccn/sn86086068/1912-04-25/ed-1/seq-4/.

**2.** "The Kitchen Cabinet," *Iowa County Democrat*, July 27, 1922, https://chroniclingamerica.loc.gov/lccn/sn86086852/1922-07-27/ed-1/seq-3/.

**3.** "Leaves and Stalks," *Grant County Herald*, June 8, 1844, https://chroniclingamerica.loc.gov/lccn/sn87082160/1844-06-08/ed-1/seq-1.

**4.** "Death in Rhubarb Leaves," *River Falls Journal*, June 1, 1876, https://chroniclingamerica.loc.gov/lccn/sn85033255/1876-06-01/ed-1/seq-3.

**5.** "Wisconsin State News," *Superior Times*, June 9, 1883, https://chroniclingamerica.loc.gov/lccn/sn85040344/1883-06-09/ed-1/seq-1.

**6.** "The Local Field," *Mineral Point Tribune*, June 10, 1886, https://chroniclingamerica.loc.gov/lccn/sn86086770/1886-06-10/ed-1/seq-1.

**7.** "Thursday," *Baraboo Weekly News*, June 7, 1917, https://chroniclingamerica.loc.gov/lccn/sn86086068/1917-06-07/ed-1/seq-5.

**8.** "Housekeepers' Helps," *Kenosha Telegraph*, July 16, 1880, https://chroniclingamerica.loc.gov/lccn/sn85033123/1880-07-16/ed-1/seq-3/.

## German-Language Recipes

**1.** Donald E. Oehlerts, *Guide to Wisconsin Newspapers 1833–1957* (Madison: State Historical Society of Wisconsin, 1958).

**2.** "Indian Pudding," *Nord Stern* (La Crosse), March 16, 1917, https://chroniclingamerica.loc.gov/lccn/sn86086186/1917-03-16/ed-1/seq-7.

**3.** "Gebrühter Pfannkuchen [Boiled Pancakes]" *Der Sonntagsbote* (Milwaukee), August 2, 1908, https://chroniclingamerica.loc.gov/lccn/sn87082455/1908-08-02/ed-1/seq-6/.

**4.** "Zwiebelkuchen [Onion Cake]" *Nord Stern* (La Crosse), July 27, 1900, https://chroniclingamerica.loc.gov/lccn/sn86086186/1900-07-27/ed-1/seq-7; "Italienischer Pfannkuchen [Italian Pancakes]," *Der Sonntagsbote* (Milwaukee), June 16, 1912, https://chroniclingamerica.loc.gov/lccn/sn87082455/ 1912-06-16/ed-1/seq-3.

**5.** "Küche und Haus [Kitchen and House]," *Der Sonntagsbote* (Milwaukee), December 4, 1910, https://chroniclingamerica.loc.gov/lccn/sn87082455/1910-12-04/ed-1/seq-7/.

## Door County Cherries

**1.** "Great Demand for Wisconsin Cherries," *Iowa County Democrat*, October 9, 1919, https://chroniclingamerica.loc.gov/lccn/sn86086852/1919-10-09/ed-1/seq-6/.

**2.** "Into Historic Wisconsin," *Baraboo Weekly News*, August 8, 1918, https://chroniclingamerica.loc.gov/lccn/sn86086068/1918-08-08/ed-1/seq-5/.

**3.** Gary Jones, "Wink Larson: Orchard in His Blood," *Door County Almanak*, no. 2, 1985: 67.

**4.** "Secrecy Clause Bill Advanced," *Vilas County News*, April 4, 1923, https://chroniclingamerica.loc.gov/lccn/sn85040613/1923-04-04/ed-1/seq-2/.

**5.** Sergio M. González, "The Cherryland Problem: Door County & Migrant Labor in the Mid-Twentieth Century," *Wisconsin Magazine of History* 106, no. 4 (Summer 2023): 31–33.

**6.** "News of the Badger State," *Vilas County News*, May 14, 1919, https://chroniclingamerica.loc.gov/lccn/sn85040613/1919-05-14/ed-1/seq-2/.

**7.** "Helpful Hints for Housewives," *Wisconsin Weekly Blade* (Madison), July 20, 1916, https://chroniclingamerica.loc.gov/lccn/sn84025842/1916-07-20/ed-1/seq-4/.

## Early Wisconsin Apiculture

**1.** Lorenzo L. Langstroth, Beehive, US Patent 9300A, dated October 5, 1852, https://patents.google.com/patent/US9300A/en.

**2.** "Beekeeping in England," *Wauwatosa News*, August 21, 1908, https://chroniclingamerica.loc.gov/lccn/sn86086499/1908-08-21/ed-1/seq-3/.

3. "Wintering Bees," *Manitowoc Pilot*, November 29, 1877, https://chroniclingamerica.loc.gov/lccn/sn85033139/1877-11-29/ed-1/seq-4.

4. "Farm Notes," *Vilas County News*, November 15, 1897, https://chroniclingamerica.loc.gov/lccn/sn85040613/1897-11-15/ed-1/seq-3.

5. "A Good Way to Winter Honey-Bees," *Wood County Reporter*, November 4, 1875, https://chroniclingamerica.loc.gov/lccn/sn85033078/1875-11-04/ed-1/seq-6/.

6. "A Good Way to Winter Honey-Bees."

7. "A Good Way to Winter Honey-Bees."

8. "Use More Honey in Your Cooking," *Wauwatosa News*, September 13, 1918, https://chroniclingamerica.loc.gov/lccn/sn86086499/1918-09-13/ed-1/seq-8/.

## Coco(a)nuts

1. "The Cocoanut. Its Importance as an Article of Commerce—Interesting Figures," *Wood County Reporter*, July 8, 1886, https://chroniclingamerica.loc.gov/lccn/sn85033078/1886-07-08/ed-1/seq-7.

2. "The Cocoanut."

3. "The Cocoanut."

4. *Southport Telegraph* (Kenosha), December 16, 1846, https://chroniclingamerica.loc.gov/lccn/sn85040303/1846-12-16/ed-1/seq-3.

5. *Superior Times*, November 25, 1871, https://chroniclingamerica.loc.gov/lccn/sn85040344/1871-11-25/ed-1/seq-4/; *Vilas County News*, September 26, 1917, https://chroniclingamerica.loc.gov/lccn/sn85040613/1917-09-26/ed-1/seq-8.

6. "Home, Farm and Garden," *Mineral Point Tribune*, October 28, 1869, https://chroniclingamerica.loc.gov/lccn/sn86086770/1869-10-28/ed-1/seq-7/.

7. "Farm, Home and Garden," *Wood County Reporter*, July 12, 1888, https://chroniclingamerica.loc.gov/lccn/sn85033078/1888-07-12/ed-1/seq-3/.

## Cottage Cheese Propaganda

1. "Value of Cottage Cheese," *Watertown News*, June 4, 1917, https://chroniclingamerica.loc.gov/lccn/sn85040720/1917-06-04/ed-1/seq-2/.

2. "Cottage Cheese, an Inexpensive Meat Substitute," *Northern Wisconsin Advertiser* (Wabeno), June 22, 1917, https://chroniclingamerica.loc.gov/lccn/sn85040705/1917-06-22/ed-1/seq-8/.

3. "Ways of Using Cottage Cheese," *Vernon County Censor*, November 20, 1918, https://chroniclingamerica.loc.gov/lccn/sn85040451/1918-11-20/ed-1/seq-7/.

4. "Ways of Using Cottage Cheese," *Iowa County Democrat*, November 21, 1918, https://chroniclingamerica.loc.gov/lccn/sn86086852/1918-11-21/ed-1/seq-7/.

## A History of Candy

**1.** *Wood County Reporter*, November 21, 1901, https://chroniclingamerica.loc.gov/lccn/sn85033078/1901-11-21/ed-1/seq-5/.

**2.** "Opening of Candy Store," *Wood County Reporter*, November 14, 1901, https://chroniclingamerica.loc.gov/lccn/sn85033078/1901-11-14/ed-1/seq-1.

**3.** Roy A. Ballinger, "A History of Sugar Marketing Through 1974," USDA Economics, Statistics, and Cooperatives Service, Agricultural Economic Report No. (AER-382), March 1978, 16, https://babel.hathitrust.org/cgi/pt?id=uiug.30112018967569&seq=24.

**4.** Mary Marshall Duffee, "The Right Thing at the Right Time," *Wisconsin Weekly Blade* (Madison), August 5, 1922, https://chroniclingamerica.loc.gov/lccn/sn84025842/1922-08-05/ed-1/seq-3/.

**5.** "The Kitchen Cabinet," *Watertown Weekly Leader*, February 13, 1914, https://chroniclingamerica.loc.gov/lccn/sn85040721/1914-02-13/ed-1/seq-3/.

## Carry Your Own Basket!

**1.** "Didn't Get What She Wanted," *River Falls Journal*, January 9, 1896, https://chroniclingamerica.loc.gov/lccn/sn85033255/1896-01-09/ed-1/seq-3.

**2.** Kat Eschner, "The Bizarre Story of Piggly Wiggly, the First Self-Service Grocery Store," *Smithsonian Magazine*, September 6, 2017, www.smithsonianmag.com/smart-news/bizarre-story-piggly-wiggly-first-self-service-grocery-store-180964708/.

**3.** "Groceteria," *Mineral Point Tribune*, September 26, 1918, https://chroniclingamerica.loc.gov/lccn/sn86086770/1918-09-26/ed-1/seq-1/.

**4.** *Iowa County Democrat*, October 17, 1918, https://chroniclingamerica.loc.gov/lccn/sn86086852/1918-10-17/ed-1/seq-5/.

**5.** "The Groceteria Co.," *Mineral Point Tribune*, October 31, 1918, https://chroniclingamerica.loc.gov/lccn/sn86086770/1918-10-31/ed-1/seq-1/.

**6.** "This and That," *Baraboo Weekly News*, August 12, 1920, https://chroniclingamerica.loc.gov/lccn/sn86086068/1920-08-12/ed-1/seq-4.

**7.** "Haus- und Landwirtschaftliches [Domestic and Agricultural News]," *Nord Stern* (La Crosse), April 6, 1900, https://chroniclingamerica.loc.gov/lccn/sn86086186/1900-04-06/ed-1/seq-7/.

## Cups of All Kinds

**1.** "Peculiarities of Etiquette," *Grant County Herald*, July 6, 1899, https://chroniclingamerica.loc.gov/lccn/sn85033133/1899-07-06/ed-1/seq-2.

**2.** *Manitowoc Pilot*, July 30, 1914, https://chroniclingamerica.loc.gov/lccn/sn85033139/1914-07-30/ed-1/seq-8/.

3. "Pressed Glass History," Vallier Goblet Collection, University of Wisconsin–Stevens Point, www3.uwsp.edu/cofac/goblet/Pages/pressed-glass-history.aspx.

4. "Fashion Ideas and Household Hints," *Odanah Star*, August 16, 1912, https://chroniclingamerica.loc.gov/lccn/sn84024927/1912-08-16/ed-1/seq-7/.

## Doctor's Orders

1. "City and County," *Manitowoc Tribune*, March 30, 1876, https://chroniclingamerica.loc.gov/lccn/sn85033153/1876-03-30/ed-1/seq-3/.

2. "Blackberry Cordial," *Wood County Reporter*, August 26, 1897, https://chroniclingamerica.loc.gov/lccn/sn85033078/1897-08-26/ed-1/seq-7/.

3. "Cooling Drinks," *Watertown Republican*, August 19, 1896, https://chroniclingamerica.loc.gov/lccn/sn85033295/1896-08-19/ed-1/seq-7/.

4. "Mince Pie Cocktails," *Vilas County News*, August 24, 1896, https://chroniclingamerica.loc.gov/lccn/sn85040613/1896-08-24/ed-1/seq-8/.

5. "Wisconsin Happenings," *Wausau Pilot*, July 27, 1922, https://chroniclingamerica.loc.gov/lccn/sn85040749/1922-07-27/ed-1/seq-5/.

6. "Many Want Permits to Prescribe Liquor," *River Falls Journal*, January 29, 1925, https://chroniclingamerica.loc.gov/lccn/sn85033255/1925-01-29/ed-1/seq-4/; "The New Enforcement Law," *Manitowoc Pilot*, July 7, 1921, https://chroniclingamerica.loc.gov/lccn/sn85033139/1921-07-07/ed-1/seq-1/.

7. "Way to Get Liquor," *Wauwatosa News*, February 6, 1920, https://chroniclingamerica.loc.gov/lccn/sn86086499/1920-02-06/ed-1/seq-1/.

8. Megan Gambino, "During Prohibition, Your Doctor Could Write You a Prescription for Booze," *Smithsonian Magazine*, October 7, 2013, www.smithsonianmag.com/history/during-prohibition-your-doctor-could-write-you-prescription-booze-180947940/.

9. "Druggists to Sell Some Beer," *Telegraph-Courier* (Kenosha), October 27, 1921, https://chroniclingamerica.loc.gov/lccn/sn85040310/1921-10-27/ed-1/seq-5/.

10. "The Housewife's Exchange," *Wausau Pilot*, August 10, 1922, https://chroniclingamerica.loc.gov/lccn/sn85040749/1922-08-10/ed-1/seq-2/.

11. "The Housewife's Exchange."

## Swiss Miss Hot Cocoa

1. Sam Roberts, "Charles Sanna, Man Behind Swiss Miss Cocoa, Dies at 101," *New York Times*, April 2, 2019, www.nytimes.com/2019/04/02/obituaries/charles-sanna-dead.html.

2. Brigit Katz, "Charles Sanna's Cocoa Packets Changed the Way We Drink Hot Chocolate," *Smithsonian Magazine*, April 5, 2019, www.smithsonianmag.com/smart-news/charles-sanna-inventor-instant-hot-cocoa-has-died-101-180971882/.

3. "History of Chocolate," *Manitowoc Pilot*, May 9, 1878, https://chroniclingamerica.loc.gov/lccn/sn85033139/1878-05-09/ed-1/seq-1.

4. "Cocoa and Chocolate," *Wausau Pilot*, May 13, 1913, https://chroniclingamerica.loc.gov/lccn/sn85040749/1913-05-13/ed-1/seq-9.

5. Chris Aadland, "The Instant Cocoa Man—But Hot Chocolate Mix Isn't This Vet's Only Accomplishment," *Wisconsin State Journal*, February 9, 2019.

6. "Hints for Your Christmas Menu," *Wauwatosa News*, December 14, 1917, https://chroniclingamerica.loc.gov/lccn/sn86086499/1917-12-14/ed-1/seq-2/.

## Tea Time

1. *Southport Telegraph* (Kenosha), December 2, 1845, https://chroniclingamerica.loc.gov/lccn/sn85040303/1845-12-02/ed-1/seq-4.

2. "Black and Green Tea," *Northern Wisconsin Advertiser* (Wabeno), May 29, 1902, https://chroniclingamerica.loc.gov/lccn/sn85040705/1902-05-29/ed-1/seq-8.

3. *Kenosha Telegraph*, August 3, 1871, https://chroniclingamerica.loc.gov/lccn/sn85033123/1871-08-03/ed-1/seq-8.

4. "Tea of Ceylon," *Wauwatosa News*, January 9, 1904, https://chroniclingamerica.loc.gov/lccn/sn86086499/1904-01-09/ed-1/seq-4.

5. *River Falls Journal*, March 10, 1910, https://chroniclingamerica.loc.gov/lccn/sn85033255/1910-03-10/ed-1/seq-7/.

6. "Excellent Tea Punch," *Iron County News*, May 1, 1915, https://chroniclingamerica.loc.gov/lccn/sn85040652/1915-05-01/ed-1/seq-3/.

## Keeping Cool with Summer Kitchens

1. "Dexterville," *Wood County Reporter*, July 8, 1886, https://chroniclingamerica.loc.gov/lccn/sn85033078/1886-07-08/ed-1/seq-8/.

2. "Special Notices," *Kenosha Telegraph*, June 1, 1876, https://chroniclingamerica.loc.gov/lccn/sn85033123/1876-06-01/ed-1/seq-8/.

3. "Milton," *Wisconsin Tobacco Reporter* (Edgerton), September 4, 1903, https://chroniclingamerica.loc.gov/lccn/sn86086586/1903-09-04/ed-1/seq-8/.

4. *Baraboo News*, May 29, 1907, https://chroniclingamerica.loc.gov/lccn/sn86086067/1907-05-29/ed-1/seq-4/; *Wisconsin Tobacco Reporter* (Edgerton), May 4, 1917, https://chroniclingamerica.loc.gov/lccn/sn86086586/1917-05-04/ed-1/seq-7/.

5. "Designed to Fit on Narrow Lot," *Eagle River Review*, July 3, 1914, https://chroniclingamerica.loc.gov/lccn/sn85040614/1914-07-03/ed-1/seq-2/.

6. "The Household," *Wauwatosa News*, October 31, 1903, https://chroniclingamerica.loc.gov/lccn/sn86086499/1903-10-31/ed-1/seq-2/.

## The Age of Aprons

1. *Wisconsin Tobacco Reporter* (Edgerton), March 17, 1899, https://chroniclingamerica.loc.gov/lccn/sn86086586/1899-03-17/ed-1/seq-4/.

2. "Neat and Durable Serving Apron Is Not Hard to Make," *Washburn Times*, January 15, 1914, https://chroniclingamerica.loc.gov/lccn/sn85040437/1914-01-15/ed-1/seq-2/.

3. "Dainty Embroidery," *Watertown Leader*, July 29, 1910, https://chroniclingamerica.loc.gov/lccn/sn85040722/1910-07-29/ed-1/seq-6/.

4. "For the House Keeper," *Vilas County News*, September 18, 1912, https://chroniclingamerica.loc.gov/lccn/sn85040613/1912-09-18/ed-1/seq-3/.

5. "Farm and Home," *Dodgeville Chronicle*, June 18, 1875, https://chroniclingamerica.loc.gov/lccn/sn85033019/1875-06-18/ed-1/seq-4/.

## Preserving Apples

1. "Fruit Trees," *Southport Telegraph* (Kenosha), October 27, 1840, https://chroniclingamerica.loc.gov/lccn/sn85040303/1840-10-27/ed-1/seq-2/.

2. "Facts for Our Farmers," *Northern Wisconsin Advertiser* (Wabeno), December 29, 1904, https://chroniclingamerica.loc.gov/lccn/sn85040705/1904-12-29/ed-1/seq-4/.

3. "Temperance," *River Falls Journal*, November 4, 1886, https://chroniclingamerica.loc.gov/lccn/sn85033255/1886-11-04/ed-1/seq-1/.

4. Jorg Augustin, Evelyn Augustin, Rena L. Cutrufelli, Steven R. Hagen, and Charlene Teitzel, "Alcohol Retention in Food Preparation," *Journal of American Dietetic Association* 92, no. 4 (April 1992): 486–487.

5. "Apple Butter," *Watertown Republican*, December 14, 1881, https://chroniclingamerica.loc.gov/lccn/sn85033295/1881-12-14/ed-1/seq-2/.

6. "Apple Butter."

7. "Apple Butter."

8. "Domestic Economy," *Watertown Republican*, December 14, 1881, https://chroniclingamerica.loc.gov/lccn/sn85033295/1881-12-14/ed-1/seq-2/.

# INDEX

Page numbers in *italics* indicate illustrations.
Entries in **bold type** indicate title of recipe.

# ABOUT THE AUTHORS

For two years, Jane Conway and Randi Julia Ramsden worked together on the National Digital Newspaper Program at the Wisconsin Historical Society. In 2019, they began researching, cooking, and writing for the "Cooking Up History" series, which appeared on the Society's website and provided the inspiration for this book. Conway has a bachelor's degree in art history from the University of Oregon, and Ramsden has a master's degree in American studies from Johannes Gutenberg University Mainz.